BRISTOL OLD VIC
Anecdotes on stage and off

BRISTOL OLD·VIC

First published in 1992 by Redcliffe Press Ltd.,
49 Park Street, Bristol

© The contributors

The Bristol office of KPMG Peat Marwick, accountants and management consultants, are delighted to have sponsored this book as part of the campaign to keep Britain's oldest working theatre open. We hope that its sales will help the Theatre Royal to go from strength to strength.

KPMG Peat Marwick

ISBN 1 872971 51 2

Typeset by Alphaset Ltd, Bristol and printed and bound
by The Longdunn Press Ltd, Bristol

CONTENTS

Message from HRH The Prince of Wales .. 5
Introduction – Mark Everett, Executive
    Director, Bristol Old Vic.............. 6
In Front of the Curtain – Tom Stoppard ... 7
The Coming of the Bristol Old Vic –
    Peter Harris 9
Robert Aldous 17
Michael Aldridge.................... 18
Jane Asher 19
June Barrie........................ 20
Christopher Benjamin................ 23
Isla Blair......................... 24
Jean Boht 25
Peter Bowles...................... 28
Adrian Bray 29
Eleanor Bron 31
Jason Connery 34
Peter Copley...................... 34
Richard Cottrell................... 36
Paul Darrow...................... 39
Paul Eddington 42
John Elvery 44
Christopher Ettridge 45
Rosemary Finnegan................. 47
Barry Foster 48
Julian Glover 49
Edward Hardwicke 51
Chris Harris 53
Louise Jameson 54
Jane Lapotaire.................... 56
Barbara Leigh-Hunt 57
Pip Mayo 59
Adrian Noble 59
Richard Pasco 61

Tim Pigott-Smith 64
Donald Pleasence 65
Amanda Redman 67
Leonard Rossiter 71
Prunella Scales 75
James Taljaard 78
Dorothy Tutin 81
Julie Walters 82
Rodney West 84
Timothy West 85
Elaine White 87
David Wood 89
Peggy Ann Wood 90
Gary Yershon 91
The Ghost of Sarah Who? 92

KENSINGTON PALACE

I need hardly say that I very much hope it will prove possible to keep the Bristol Old Vic, the oldest working theatre in the country, in business for the benefit of the local community.

Our theatres are a vital part of our cultural heritage and, more importantly, of our children's education. Without theatres such as the Bristol Old Vic, with its renowned Education Department, it will become impossible for young people to have access to the major works of past and present theatre. Lack of resources threatens in particular the ability of our theatres to produce larger cast plays – including many of Shakespeare's works – as well as many of the admirable educational projects which make such a contribution to learning in local schools.

I wish the Bristol Old Vic Theatre Club every success in their difficult struggle.

INTRODUCTION

This book of theatrical memories was born out of the desire to keep them alive within the continuing tradition of the Bristol Old Vic's activities in Britain's oldest working theatre – the Bristol Theatre Royal. The Bristol office of a major firm of accountants and a Bristol publisher both saw that their famous local theatre was threatened by financial difficulties which were not of its making, and were determined to help. The result is this book. It records some of the many experiences and anecdotes, funny and sad, of that large and distinguished cast of actors and actresses who have worked with the Bristol Old Vic since its founding in 1946 as the then new Arts Council's first regional subsidised theatre company.

The proceeds from sales of this book will go towards keeping the Bristol Old Vic open and maintaining it not only as a great theatre company in which future generations of players can develop their craft, but also as a vibrant and entertaining cultural asset for the people of Bristol, Avon and far beyond.

On behalf of all of us at the Bristol Old Vic I must record my thanks to Jeffrey Hordle and his colleagues at KPMG Peat Marwick for sponsoring the project, to Redcliffe Press for developing the idea, to Richard Bladon for his great patience with coordinating the motley efforts of a disparate group of people between the covers of one book, to His Royal Highness the Prince of Wales for the strength of his support for the Bristol Old Vic, to Tom Stoppard for his generous comments in the foreword, to Christopher Robinson for his invaluable help and permission to use material from the University of Bristol's theatre collection, to the staff of the Bristol Old Vic and to all the many actors and actresses who took the time and trouble to show their love and support for a great theatre company by recording some of their experiences with it.

Mark Everett, Executive Director, Bristol Old Vic.

IN FRONT OF THE CURTAIN

Tom Stoppard

To the Romans *alumnus* meant a nursling or foster child, and *alma mater* was the nourishing mother. It is usual to associate the Latin tags with school or college but I have never been in any doubt that I am an alumnus of Bristol and more particularly of two institutions housed a stone's throw from each other. The first of my nourishing mothers was the *Western Daily Press* and the second was the Bristol Old Vic.

On this axis between Baldwin Street and King Street – later redirected across the City Centre to the *Evening World,* and later again towards Bridewell and the old *Evening Post* building – my life turned and was shaped for ever after.

So it is not a dry exercise for me, this business of writing the bit of the book which everybody skips. I was a junior reporter when I entered the Theatre Royal for the first time, and it still feels more as if it entered me.

Now that I am more interviewed against than interviewing, the question "Why did you choose to write for the theatre?" is often the first one to be asked, and I have become adept at answering it in a theoretical vein as one does: the unique event, the live experience, the mysterious chemistry which makes the thing more than the sum of its parts (or sometimes less, which one doesn't dwell on) and the rest. But a truer answer might begin, "Well, I was living in Bristol at the time and I got to hanging about the Theatre Royal . . ."

It was not that those Old Vic seasons of the Fifties were the first theatre I had seen, not even in Bristol; junior reviewers were familiar with the amateur theatre and sometimes were honoured with second-week tickets for the Little or the Hippodrome. But the Theatre Royal was my first backstage, and if you're going to catch the bug, I think that's where you catch it.

For some years while my ambitions were still in journalism, many of my friends were at the Old Vic. And on one terrifying night my two lives intersected when, for the purposes of writing an article, I made my debut – and my swansong – on the boards of the Theare Royal, in a play by G. B. Shaw no less. I had no lines but I had stagefright as if it were my responsibility to make the show "Shavian". Togged out as an Arab, I held my wooden dagger at the throat of Emrys James and got off without knocking over the scenery.

I am grateful to have had the experience now because I claim it as my symbolic credential for this appearance in front of the curtain. I, too, trod the boards. Much has happened to the front-of-house since then but the boards are as they have always been and so is the view from them. That arc encompasses what has been for me the Platonic Theatre, unchallenged for – good heavens! – nearly forty years. (Come to think of it, years ago a stage manager at the National Theatre introduced himself to me as the infant whom I babysat while his parents were out acting in King Street.)

One must beware of sounding like the old-timer who said of the Atlantic, "Ah yes, but you should have seen it back then." Well, you should have, and there will be someone to say it again years from now so long as we value the capability to inspire. The fabric of the oldest and most beautiful theatre in England is now safe, but it is the life inside the building which makes the Theatre Royal inspirational, and that is the reason for this book.

THE COMING OF THE BRISTOL OLD VIC

Peter Harris

The arrival of the Old Vic Company at the Theatre in 1946 meant that a resident company had to fit itself into what had been a touring theatre. Every possible part was adapted to accommodate the newcomers and provide enough space to rehearse the next play and build the sets whilst performing the current one. The permanent staff came mostly from the old Prince's Theatre with T. C. P. Hickson as theatre manager. Box office staff, electricians, stage hands, carpenter, wardrobe mistress and even the stage door keeper all came from the Prince's. They had been accustomed to ways of the "commercial theatre" where shows moved in for one or two weeks and then moved on. The staff were used to this at the Royal for the theatre had worked as a touring date since 1943.

Now all was changed. There were no perks for working on Saturday night "Get-Outs", the presence of a permanent Stage Director meant that carpenters and stage staff were fully occupied. It is little wonder that the Old Vic staff became accustomed to hearing the litany, "We didn't do it like that at the Prince's."

1946 was not the best time to set up a new repertory company. Everything was in short supply. The soft wood to build scenery required a permit, clothes were rationed, essentials like canvas for back cloths and flats was almost unobtainable. By dint of various devious means essential materials were acquired. The local ships' chandlers were able to supply new rope, pulley blocks and other essentials. They also stocked a form of canvas known as "PS 208" which could be used for covering flats. The London Old Vic sent loads of old scenery and Sadler's Wells chipped in. Sadly, most of the flats were too tall, twenty feet high when only fourteen feet could be used. Treads and rostrums that were worn were very useful and could be repaired. Soon a stock of usable scenery was assembled and by the second season Alan Barlow had a book containing the details of all that was available. Designing a set for a new production became a test of ingenuity – balancing what was available with what could be built and somehow fudging the odd bits and pieces.

The Company did have an allocation of clothing coupons but there were never enough. A production where all the men needed tights could use up most of the coupons before even getting to the costumes.

Again, the Old Vic Wardrobe helped out but then it was discovered that furnishing fabrics could be obtained without coupons and many a chintz curtain fabric was used to make 16th century costumes.

The opening of the Theatre School made further demands on space, the Director's office being at the top of the stairs on the OP side of the stage on the same level as the fly floor. Students had to pass under the stage to get there. The same shortages affected the school. An early school end-of-year production of "The Yellow Jacket" used parts from the fuselage of a surplus Horsa glider to make the temple roof. The one class room over the fruit store was hardly adequate and the St. Nicholas schoolroom provided extra space (in the playground if fine!).

The stage was a museum piece and was not an efficient place to mount modern plays. The only asset was the lighting consol which was as modern a system as could be had in 1946. All the lights were permanently fixed on the grid and a lighting rehearsal involved two or three hours of precarious balancing by Ernie Peppin, the electrician, on the top of a ladder as he focussed the spots and changed the colours. All the cloths and other items which had to be "flown" were hoisted up by sheer brute force by the stage staff and tied off on the cleat rail on the fly-floor. A big scene change could result in the fly floor looking like the deck of a sailing ship rounding Cape Horn as the staff heaved on ropes and slackened off others to complete the change.

The stage itself presented problems, having a rake from front to back but originally also a dip towards the OP side (said to be the result of an elephant belonging to a circus standing on that side for two or three months). When a new floor was eventually laid, this depression was removed. There was never enough room for extra scenery if there was a number of scene changes. Often flats from Act One had to be stacked in the entrance to the paint dock thus annoying the painters. On one occasion a set of flats from the London Old Vic arrived covered in flock wallpaper. Before they could be used the paper had to be stripped and during performances some of the actors helped, clearly feeling that it was a form of occupational therapy. The various trap doors were needed from time to time but they were liable to stick and the back one, used for "Cinderella's" coach in the 1948 pantomime, stuck during one matinee and could not be used again.

Sound effects were primitive. The famous thunder run over the ceiling of the auditorium was used for a while in the production of "King Lear" in the second season but the vibration caused by the iron cannon balls running down the trough threatened the plaster ceiling and so the traditional thunder sheet was used thereafter. Recorded music could be played from "78" discs on a twin turntable amplifier

10

known as the "panotrope" ("pan" for short). Cutting in at the precise point on the disc was always a headache for the Stage Manager.

The simple business of living presented problems for the staff. There were several cafés in Baldwin Street, but on Sundays the only place offering a meal was the New Palace Cinema. The local pubs did

The theatre as it was a hundred years ago.

not provide much more than a pickled egg or a bag of crisps and they were open only from 10.30am to 2.30pm and 6pm to 10pm. (Hence Newton Blick's comment when the "Italian Straw Hat" finished at the early time of 9.20 – "There's a significant message in this play – Curtain Down 9.20, in the pub 9.30 – half-an-hour's drinking time") There was also Balch's Café in King Street (usually known as "Hell's Kitchen") where thick mugs of tea and pork pies and buns could be purchased.

The Old Vic staff were not overpaid. The ASMs and assistant painter received about £3.00 a week. The actors were not much better off and the highest salary paid to an actor in 1946–48 was £60.00 a week to Margaretta Scott. The "take" for a Full House (every seat sold) in 1948 was about £140. It is hardly surprising that the theatre needed a subsidy and that everything was done as economically as possible.

The great success of the Bristol Old Vic Company in those early

years was due to the remarkable devotion of all who worked for the company. This showed itself in endless hours of overtime, enduring cold and physical discomfort, and taking endless pains to get something exactly as Hugh Hunt or Denis Carey wanted it. An expression of thanks or appreciation from them was considered to make it all worth while. It is not surprising that many of those from the early seasons went on to achieve success in various parts of the theatre.

On Sunday August 17th 1952 the Theatre Royal was the venue for the first West of England television drama production "Tess of the d'Urbervilles". In those days plays were transmitted live and usually from the stage where they were performed to a live audience. This was a special production and was part of a series of programmes transmitted after the opening of the new transmitter at Wenvoe. It formed part of the "Armchair Theatre" series which went out about 7.30 on Sunday evenings. The play was cast by the BBC with Barbara Jefford, a local actress of some fame, in the leading role. The producer was Owen Reed of the BBC's West Region. The theatre was closed for the summer and the Autumn Old Vic season began on September 1st. This meant that the stage staff and the Old Vic production team were available for the rehearsals and the performance. The settings were designed and painted by Patrick Robertson who was a designer with the company.

Of course, this new-fangled television was something few people in Bristol, even at the BBC, knew very much about. The actual transmission would be handled by the Outside Broadcast unit from Cardiff and local BBC staff were enlisted as well. The sound effects man from Whiteladies Road arrived on a motor-bicycle and sidecar with a few tools of his trade clutched in his hands. The local Signal and Telegraph Inspector from British Rail brought an authentic railway telegraph instrument.

The stage staff and the Old Vic stage management built the sets, changed the scenes where necessary and operated the lighting switchboard. Relatively few extra lights were needed.

To the delight of the theatre staff a BBC canteen was set up in the main bar and hot drinks and snacks were available free of charge during the four days of rehearsal – an unheard of luxury. It made a change from the primitive "brew-ups" on the paint dock gas ring and the usual chipped mugs. Even more surprising was the fact that work

Opposite: above *A 1940s interior. During the war, the theatre came close to being sold for warehousing; a public appeal saved the day, and CEMA (the Council for the Encouragement of Music and the Arts) took on the lease.*
Below *Set for "The Provok'd Wife", 1950. New seating disguised the need for major work on the fabric of the building.*

The theatre in the mid-1950s after interior refurbishment. Exterior improvements and the new backstage area would follow in 1972.

finished at a reasonable hour each day (that is, before the pubs shut) and it was not necessary to work all night.

The cameras were set up in the auditorium so that viewers would get the view of the stage as seen by the live audience. The actors arrived and all the equipment was tested. A walk-through and a final dress rehearsal, and all was ready.

The stage management were enthralled at being able to stand at the door of the control van, parked in the Rackhay and watch what was happening on the stage on the monitor set. Bob Harris, one of the ASMs, was sent in to make faces at the camera for the amusement of the others.

The play was in three acts with the normal intervals but there was a scene change in Act 2. Any delay was avoided by building the two small sets side by side and simply switching the camera from one to the other.

Finally the audience began to arrive. It was an invited audience representing the great and good of the city and dinner jackets were obligatory for the men. The auditorium looked normal except for the cameras and some extra lights. Precise timing was of the essence and dead on cue the curtain went up and the stage staff were able to watch the view of it doing so from the auditorium on the monitor screen in the prompt corner (something they had never seen before). The performance carried on smoothly (though all backstage were aware that the slightest hitch would be seen by hundreds of thousands of viewers). It was a slight shock to the audience when, in the second act, the scene switched from one set to the next and one of the ASMs wandered across in full view to extinguish the candles and collect a couple of props. Obviously the viewers could not see this, but it took a moment for some of the audience to realise this.

At last it was over with the usual curtain calls, the credits rolled and everybody relaxed. The theatre staff tidied up and removed the loose props before getting ready to go to the party. The stage management went in their working clothes and boarded a bus at the Centre for the BBC. When they presented themselves at the door the commissionaire was reluctant to let them in since everbody else had been wearing dinner jackets or lounge suits. However, an imposing gentleman appeared who ordered that they be let in. He was the Head of Television Drama, no less. At the party in Studio One there was a feeling of relief that the new experience was over.

Peter Harris was a voluntary unpaid stage hand at King Street in the years after the Second World War.

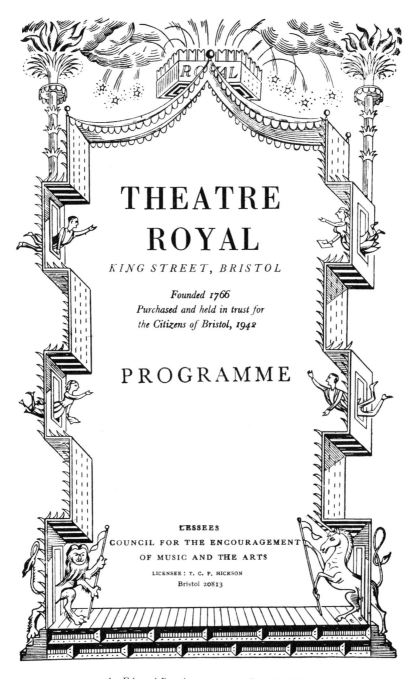

THEATRE
ROYAL

KING STREET, BRISTOL

Founded 1766
Purchased and held in trust for
the Citizens of Bristol, 1942

PROGRAMME

LESSEES
COUNCIL FOR THE ENCOURAGEMENT
OF MUSIC AND THE ARTS

LICENSEE: T. C. P. HICKSON
Bristol 20813

An Edward Bawden programme from the 1940s.

ROBERT ALDOUS

My story dates from a BOV production of " 'Tis Pity She's a Whore" at the Little Theatre in 1968.

Two fathers (Florio and Donado – Norman Henry and myself) are "arranging" a marriage in Florio's house at the back of the set, which is an open street. We are disturbed by the commotion caused by a sword fight. We emerge from the house and Florio has the line:

"What mean these sudden broils so near my doors?"

Instead, on this particular occasion, Norman utters the Spoonerism:

"What mean these sudden boils so near my drawers?"

I have never before or since seen an entire cast not just corpse, but collapse with laughter. The show stopped!

FRANK SHIPSIDES – 1977 –

MICHAEL ALDRIDGE

In the late Sixties, I think, I'm hopeless at dates, I was playing Archie Rice in John Osborne's "The Entertainer".

I was resting in my dressing room at the Theatre Royal after the matinée when a very elderly man in a shabby, tight-fitting brown overcoat, a brown Homburg hat and brightly-polished boots, came nervously in, carrying a large plastic bag.

"I caught your act at the matinée last week", he said, "and frankly Sir, I feel you should get some better material."

I tried to explain that I was an actor and the front cloth excerpts from Archie's act were intentionally corny. He shook his head sadly in disbelief and out of the plastic bag produced three large volumes and put them on my dressing table. "I'm offering you, Sir, my gag books! They're all cross-indexed and very complete. Mothers-in-law for instance or curates. You can look them all up and choose. Only five hundred pounds!"

18

We spent ten minutes together looking through the books. Every entry was carefully and beautifully written in a neat copper-plate hand. The jokes were awful and as I was earning only fifteen pounds a week and was supporting a baby and a pregnant wife – I had to tell him I couldn't afford to buy them. The little old man gathered up the books and went to the door and said rather sadly, "No Sir, I don't believe you could!"

Shamefully, I have forgotten his name and, sadly, the gag books have gone forever I expect.

JANE ASHER

The Bristol Old Vic has a very special place in my heart. I first went there at the age of 20 and spent, on and off, two extremely happy years there.

It would be desperately sad if it were to close as it, rightly, has a reputation for excellence and for a fine contribution to the British Theatre.

Jane Asher as Juliet in the BOV "Romeo and Juliet", November, 1966.

19

JUNE BARRIE

When John David, then assistant director to Val May, summoned me to the theatre one winter's morning in January 1972 to take part in Brecht's "Fears and Miseries of the Third Reich", I couldn't have guessed that I'd still be there 10 years or so later. They turned out to be 10 years of the very best acting opportunities any actor could have hoped for.

Miraculously, I survived the artistic directorships of Val May, Richard Cottrell and John David between 1972 and 1983 and when I returned in '86 to play Mrs. Malaprop, I met Paul Unwin who later asked me to do Mrs. Gascoigne in "The Daughter-in-Law".

The O'Toole season in 1973 was, for me, the most exciting of all. I was lucky enough to be included in the "ensemble" which included among others, Marie Kean, Edward Hardwicke, Nigel Stock and Penelope Wilton. It turned out to be the most successful season in the history of the Old Vic. By this time, of course, Peter had become an international star and the houses were full to capacity – even the matinées – despite an electricians' strike during some very cold weather. We did "Uncle Vanya", "Plunder" and "The Apple Cart". His amazing affinity with the audience was an object-lesson to all there and the laughter from the audience during "Plunder" was the loudest and most prolonged I've ever heard!

Shortly after came my chance to play Lilian Baylis in a centenary production. We were asked to do a midnight matinée for the National Theatre Company, concurrently doing "The Tempest" at the Bristol Hippodrome. They came round afterwards – John Geilgud, Cyril Cusack and others – and stayed for a champagne reception at what must have been 3am!

All sorts of strangers seemed to find their way round to the dressing-room after the show. Once, I remember, I was busy removing all the padding and make-up when the door was flung open and an almost phantom like figure appeared, in full evening dress with long flowing white hair and a silk scarf to match, saying "The spirit of that woman was present in this theatre tonight!" – and then disappeared. I was so convinced he must have been a ghost, that, throwing pride to the wind, I flung a scarf over my pinned-up hair, snatched my handbag and raced for my last 'bus!

I suppose one of the most hilarious moments for the company came when the safety curtain descended unaccountably during "Oh! What a Lovely War". We were lined up downstage doing the number "Oh, we don't want to lose you, but we think you ought to go" – flinging

June Barrie as Stevie Smith in "Stevie", 1980.

our legs alternately to right and left, when suddenly we found ourselves staring at SAFETY CURTAIN, the wrong way round, and the audience slowly but surely disappearing from view!

Apparently the effigy of the Kaiser had been inadvertently plonked up against the handle which operated the safety curtain mechanism by the actor concerned, who had then sauntered off for a coffee till his next scene – entirely oblivious to the havoc he'd left behind. However, we kept going until the stage management did the decent thing and brought it up again!

Twice, during the years I was with the company, I inadvertently inspired audience participation. In "When We Are Married", I played the long-suffering Annie Parker who had decided after 25 years of domination by her pompous, self-satisfied husband, to let him know in a lengthy speech just how she felt about him. After a thunderstruck silence, he says something like "Annie, love, how long have you felt like this?" to which her response is (after a well-timed pause): "TWENTY-FIVE YEARS". It usually brought the house down, but on this one evening I let the pause go on a bit too long and a voice from the audience said the line for me! I could do no other than, "Yes, that's right, 25 years!"

When the same thing happened during a matinée of Arthur Miller's "All My Sons", though, it really didn't help! In this wonderful play the husband commits suicide after a terrible revelation about his past and a frightful family upset. It's at the end of the play and the wife, whom I was playing, and the eldest son, are in the garden when the shot rings out. Her response was to say his name several times over in tragic disbelief, "Joe, Joe, Joe, Joe, Joe, . . ." We had agonised long and hard over the best way to do this and it had seemed to be working – until this fateful afternoon when, at the end of my "Joe, Joe, Joe . . ." a voice floated up from the largely elderly audience with: "I'm afraid he gone far beyond recall!" There was no answer to that!

June Barrie

CHRISTOPHER BENJAMIN

In all probability the Theatre Royal, Bristol was the second theatre I ever went to. As a child I went on an annual visit to the Frank Maddox pantos at the Theatre Royal, Bath, then as a schoolboy in Warminster I started going on school visits to the Bristol Old Vic and my enthusiasm for the theatre was kindled!

Among my favourite memories is Miles Malleson in his own translation of Molière's "Le Bourgeois Gentilhomme" entitled "The Prodigious Snob" and the most favourite of all – Denis Carey's great production of "Two Gentlemen of Verona".

Some years after seeing this production (twice) when I was a 19-year-old amateur actor with the Octagon Players of Bath, I was playing the Gravedigger in "Hamlet" and suddenly and triumphantly brought into my performance at the dress rehearsal a piece of business remembered from Newton Blick's performance where he slowly and meticulously peeled an apple and eventually threw the apple away and ate the last piece of peel. It brought the house down at Bristol but received a gasp and nervous titters in our rehearsal room for our director was playing Hamlet himself. He was Edward Stanley, who was then director of the Old Vic Theatre School and the business was immediately cut and I received my first lesson in professionalism!

Later in my early years as a professional it was, of course, a great thrill to be a member of the company at the Bristol Old Vic from 1962 until the end of the exciting Shakespeare Quatercentenary Tour in 1964, and I have enjoyed returning on several occasions since, most recently in the 1987 production of "The Doctor's Dilemma".

Christopher Benjamin

ISLA BLAIR

I was lucky enough to play in 10 productions at the BOV in the heady days of 1974 and '75. There were many productions in those years in all three theatres – the place literally was humming. Each lunch-time members of the public would come in for lunch and a chat with actors and crew, often on the floor as it got crowded. Opinions would be exchanged about current productions, excited murmurings about forthcoming ones. People in the city seemed eager to talk to actors and were proud of the theatre and the standard of productions. There was a feeling that we all shared in the success of the Vic, staff, actors and audience alike – there was no "them and us".

I remember playing Heloise in 'Abelard and Heloise" one matinée to a party of fifth-formers from a local school. They had been given a tour of the theatre (and unbeknown to their chaperones or us, a tour of the local pubs as well). During the famous naked love scene (which was innocent and tender and not sexy at all) there was much cat-calling, whistling and giggling. You're very exposed standing naked on stage, the stuff of nightmares and I think my entire body blushed! However, I grabbed a dressing gown from somewhere and asked the audience if they'd like to go home or could we continue without the heckling? To my astonishment silence fell and we finished the performance.

The next day flowers arrived with letters of apology from the, by now, hungover schoolchildren, who promised to come and see the play again. They did.

Seven years later I was playing in "The Browning Version" and after one show a young man came backstage and reminded me of the "Abelard and Heloise" incident – he'd been one of the hecklers but had turned into a committed theatregoer. I was really chuffed! I wonder how he, and many like him, feel about the possible demise of their theatre?

JEAN BOHT

I had several goals in mind when I began my career in 1962 and these were to work at the Bristol Old Vic, The English Stage Company, and the National Theatre.

Well it's 1964 and I've made the first step of my ambitions – Val May has offered me a season – two super parts to start and the rest when plays have been decided. The 1963 company is touring Europe with Val in charge and he will return to Bristol once he has seen them on their way and plan the remainder of the Old Vic season.

This was to be my first experience away from home – I had begun my career at the Liverpool Playhouse, my native city, only two-and-a-half years previously and although I had indeed appeared with the English Stage Company, it was rather short-lived – the ill-fated but fantastic production of "St. Joan of the Stockyards" at the Queen's which ran for only three of its projected 11 weeks. Never mind. And I had stayed with friends in London for this brief West End appearance. I didn't know anyone at all in Bristol so kindly Val Lorraine took me in, as she has so many Bristol actors and musicians, until I could find a flat – which I did at only £3.50 a week overlooking Clifton College.

Was there ever a more beautiful theatre in the world than the Old Vic – green and gold and magical? I had visions of living out my life and work here and at the wondrous salary of £25 a week – I had never hoped I could earn so much. Of course, I wasn't actually going to appear in that hallowed place just yet – I was scheduled to play at the "Little", but never mind, my turn would surely come. After all, I had seen the big chart on the wall in the office. Actors could appear in two plays at once by running across the road as 'twere – perhaps changing costumes and wigs as they ran. Oh! the joy, the excitement, I could see it all.

Of course, Old Vic actors were all tall, blonde and beautiful by repute and I couldn't help being born small, dark and, well, perky. The wardrobe department were rather disappointed to find I couldn't fit into Barbara Jefford's old costumes as they talked glowingly of her many performances. I felt I had let them down and I hadn't even started rehearsals yet.

My first part as a murderess in a French thriller called "Isabelle" was a bit of a challenge but my big moment came when the detective accused me of the crime and I had to go into hysterics. John Franklyn Robbins was very helpful to me at our technical dress rehearsal, "Go for it", he said, "just jump off that high diving board and don't think about trying to swim". And I did – boy oh boy – no-one had seen hysterics like it! There had been talk of a possible West End transfer but sadly this never materialised. In fact, the audiences didn't materialise either and those thousands queueing up were all going to see the Rolling Stones, not us, never mind.

Everyone was now looking forward to the next production, "Dandy Dick" a marvellously funny Pinero farce which we all knew well and which would have the audiences rolling in the aisles. It was to be an "all star" Old Vic cast with Harold Innocent, Patricia Brake, Ann

Morrison, Edith MacArthur, and me of course. We experienced a few problems with the furniture on the dress rehearsal – heavy Victorian tables and chairs filled the little stage and spilled onto the apron. It wasn't called the "Little" for nothing but, never mind, we all knew it was a hysterical, laugh-a-line play and rehearsals had been hilarious.

A strange silence greeted our efforts on the opening night – not a titter twitter; no gales of joyous laughter sweeping us on. The end was a positive relief as despair followed despair and we fell at last into the pub to drown out the disaster – our director seemed to have disappeared. John Franklyn Robbins again came to the rescue. "We can't see you, you see – it looks like a Punch and Judy show. When you stand beind the furniture you look as though you've got no legs and when you sit on anything in the front you look all head and feet. Get rid of the furniture; stop thinking it's so funny and let the audience enjoy the situations – you'll get the laughs." So we did, and we did – eventually. Early lessons in farce playing – it's drama really.

With all this I had forgotten there were only a few days left of my initial contract. Val May had flown in one night apparently, seen productions at the Little and the Old Vic, and flown out again without speaking to anyone – he was infamously shy. No cast lists had appeared – I was a failure, he didn't want me to stay, no use Harold Innocent trying to comfort me with "there must be some mistake". He and the others had a contract for the year anyway. There was no mistake. Yes, I am short, dark and only perky! How I mourned the lack of those six inches and the blonde hair, that must be it.

I packed my bags and left on the midnight train after the last performance, tearfully waving to my new friends – it was strange no-one in the administration office had my cards and fare ready but, mine not to reason why, they could follow on. Anyway, David Scase back in Liverpool had already offered me several good parts if I would return and he was excited about a young actor called Anthony Hopkins in his company, so I went in to see him the day after. "What are you looking so miserable about," he grunted, "you'd better make up your mind what you're going to do – your agent has been on – Bristol's going potty wanting to know where you are and why have you left". The cast lists had finally gone up and I was needed after all, but because I had a two-week break no-one had bothered to let me know.

Suddenly I became confident again, arrogant even and compared the roles on offer – Liverpool's were better, so that's where I stayed.

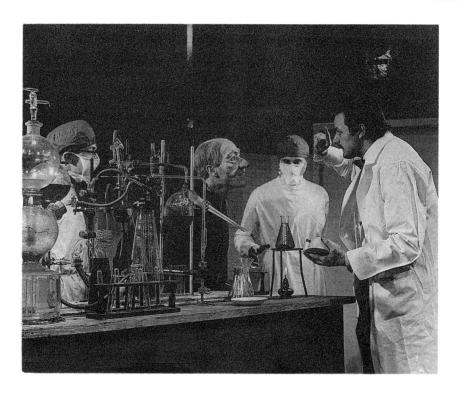

Peter Bowles in "The Happy Haven", 1960.

PETER BOWLES

I don't know of an actor who has played Bristol (meaning the Old Vic) who doesn't consider it his spiritual home.

I know I do, and I am incredulous at the thought that it could be closed down. My feelings about the Old Vic are so strong that in times of despair (usually it's the middle of the night) I have been known to drive to Bristol just to stand outside the theatre and receive fresh heart and then drive back to London.

I did one season at Bristol 1959/60, played an 80-year-old butler to the 20-year-old leading lady, fell in love and have been married to her for over 30 years now. Leonard Rossiter, Peter Jeffrey, Annette Crosbie, Patrick Garland, Robin Phillips and my so-talented wife, Susan Bennett, were all members for that season, and the friendships forged all those years ago have never been forgotten.

Actors love the Old Vic, its atmosphere and sense of continuity. The presence of all the famous names over the past 250 years is felt by every actor when he walks through the stage door. A presence, I might say, that is there not just in the theatre but in the cobbled streets around and the historic pubs of the little harbour.

Every actor will tell you that it has the best stage-audience relationship in the whole wide world. There is nothing to beat it. If you can't hold an audience at the Bristol Old Vic you won't do it anywhere else, I can assure you.

I could have told you of the funny things that happened back stage – during a show, etc – but they can happen anywhere, at any theatre. I wanted to tell you how much I and many other actors love the Bristol Old Vic and we would feel a shame and deep sorrow were it to be closed.

Good Luck.

ADRIAN BRAY

I was a deputy stage manager at the theatre from March 1989 to June 1990. Probably my most enjoyable task during my time at the Old Vic was driving the Cadillac onstage during performances of "The Man Who Had All The Luck" by Arthur Miller. This beautiful car was 50 years-old and weighed two tons but still ran smoothly and was a joy to handle. The car was parked at the back of the stage, pointing towards the audience, behind big garage doors, and at the first scene change it was my job to switch on the engine, put the headlights to main beam and drive down the rake onto two inspection ramps so actor Iain Glen could slide underneath and pretend to be fixing the engine.

Whatever the audience thought of the effect of the scene-change it was nothing compared to the joy I had at illuminating the entire auditorium and seeing from behind the wheel 650 faces wide-eyed and open-mouthed saying "Is that a real car driving right towards us?"

Needless to say, one matinée the engine failed to start and the stage crew had to man-handle the enormous machine into position. At the interval the question was asked. "Can it be fixed for this evening?" to which the only possible answer was, "I don't know, but I know a

29

The greatly loved Newton Blick, here seen as Speed in "The Two Gentlemen of Verona", 1952.

man who does!" The AA duly arrived and, much to the mechanic's bemusement, he was led onstage while the technicians went about the job of re-setting for the evening performance and was shown the huge car. It only took him a few minutes to locate a wire that had become detached from the starter motor and he put the Cadillac back in working order.

The AA's trip to the theatre was reported next day in *The Times*.

And did everyone think that the delightful high-pitched stammering voice that was the hallmark of Derek Nimmo's comedy shows on television was an act? Not a bit of it.

One evening Mr. Nimmo came to see a performance of "Plaza Suite" with David Harries and Marcia Warren, with a view to taking the show on one of his foreign tours. After the performance, while Derek was talking with the actors in their dressing rooms, the local wheel-clampers were doing their bit to encourage Bristol theatregoers by clamping cars late on a Saturday night.

Seeing that they were approaching the stage door area I shouted up to the dressing rooms. "Derek, is this old Citröen yours, because if it is, it's about to be clamped". To which the reply came in the voice we all know and love. "Er no, m-mine's the b-blue Rolls-Royce".

ELEANOR BRON

I can think of funny things and frightening things (any first night), and falling headlong over a cable as I ran, late, to take my place to rehearse the party scene in "The Card" (The Card" itself, a memory-mine of incidents, alterations, disasters – the classic tale of a musical opening "out of town"). I can think of before and after the rebuilding of the theatre, I can think of before and behind the scenes.

Most of my memories of time spent in King Street are pretty golden – time after television, three nights a week live – which I hoped I was putting to good use by learning my craft as I practised it, having failed to go to drama school. The delight of being in a musical – two! "The Boyfriend" and "The Card" – without necessarily being all that musical, but revelling in the boost that music gives and the heady atmosphere of dedication and punishing hard work that dancers always generate. On the last night of "The Boyfriend" my first and only experience of what it feels like to stop the show, with Liz Power in the duet "Poor Little Pierrot". At that period there could have been no happier substitute for school – a chance to play a wide swing of

parts, from Ayckbourn to Ibsen, to a loving and loyal audience, who watched their favourites with a proud, possessive almost parental affection. Jack and Lily Boyes came to every OAP matinée, having spent, it seemed, their entire combined pensions on boxes of chocolates for me and Gwyneth Powell. I retaliated with one of my legendary cheesecakes. We exchanged letters and cards and I still speak to Lily on the phone and visit her when I can.

So – select one memory – the one that stays. Doing "Duet for One", by Tom Kempinski, sadly to rather sparse houses – the usually faithful audiences put off, perhaps, by the subject: six sessions of analysis between a celebrated violinist, stricken at the height of her career by MS, and her psychiatrist. The violinist, Stephanie, a highly intelligent woman, racketed about in a sophisticated wheelchair, and expressed her grief and shock, her feelings of loneliness, of pain and despair at being felled, out of the blue, with perception and irony; but audiences often took a while to respond to her sharp, witty comments; many were cowed perhaps by her situation and her disability.

One night the respectful silence that greeted the early scenes was broken by high-pitched uncanny sounds that might have been laughter, but so strange. The audience shifted uneasily, and I and my colleague wondered if we were in for a disturbed evening. We went on, growing a little nervous as the noise showed no sign of abating. I could make out that the box, stage right was in use, which was itself unusual with a small house. Gradually, audience and actors relaxed; we all adjusted to the situation; and I began to realise that the laughs were not random, as they had seemed at first; nor were they nervous attempts to deal with a painful situation; they followed always after some especially acute insight into the horror of Stephanie's situation; on the contrary, for the first time they were laughs of delighted, personal recognition; someone was actually saying out loud all those thoughts that the laughter had no way to express.

Only as we took our curtain calls could we see that among several people in the box one, tiny, was almost falling out of his wheelchair, in his efforts to make us see his wild applause and make us understand his release and his joy at hearing someone say for him so many of the things that his life left unsaid. By the time I got through the pass-door, in the hope of meeting the group – I learned that they had come from a hospital for the handicapped – they had gone away on their bus.

It was a strange and haunting demonstration for me of the power and the purpose of theatre. An unconnected event 10 years later related to the same play and demonstrated the same power. I was in a restaurant in London and a man who had been at the next table came up to me on his way out, almost reluctantly, and apologising for the intrusion. He was not a theatregoer, not a fan and could not remember why he went to see "Duet for One", but he had never forgotten the evening and the experience it had given him; he felt he had to thank me.

I feel the same about the Bristol Old Vic and its importance to the community and the country.

JASON CONNERY

I was playing D'Artagnan in "The Three Musketeers." All of us in the cast were swashing a mean buckle – and then our wigs arrived.

My wig was gorgeous and made me look like Krystle (with apologies to Linda Evans) in "Dynasty". The make-up lady was justifiably proud of this creation . . . I hated it.

I re-arranged it. Now that was something like – neanderthal springs to mind. She hated it and re-arranged it.

It was a nightly occurence. We did, however, remain friends throughout. God knows how she put up with me.

PETER COPLEY

In June, 1944 the Theatre Royal had just had a welcome war-time re-opening: there was dirt everywhere, dust in the air, and the dressing rooms were filthy, but the building was still magical. Once again the audience was passing under the street canopy, through an entrance, now an outside wall where production photos are displayed, and then along a tunnel-like passage to the back of the stalls, in fact directly through the control box and lighting grid of the present New Vic. We were playing a delicate French play by Jean-Jaques Bernard, "Madeleine", so hushed that the sound of an actor placing a tea-cup on a saucer rose above the spoken word. As the cast relaxed one sunny afternoon in Victoria Square (we had digs in the then shabby Clifton) a man dashed up. "Have you heard," he said, "London's been devasted by these new bombs with wings." That was the beginning of the doodlebugs, the V1s.

Well, now the Bristol Old Vic has the Coopers' Hall and two well-equipped theatres (the New Vic lamentably closed). I am 76 and my joy and pride is that over the last 11 years, at the end of my working life, I have appeared with the Bristol Old Vic in 23 productions – it has been an extended experience with marvellous people in a marvellous theatre such as the Theatre Royal in which a permanent company is allowed to flourish. It must continue.

"The Second Mrs. Tanqueray", 1948.

RICHARD COTTRELL

The letter requested me to send "some memory of your time at the Bristol Old Vic" and a handwritten attachment asked if "you might have an amusing little anecdote or two."

Well, I daresay I have but, I don't feel it's the moment for amusing anecdotes at this point in the BOV's history, and the memory I have of my time as director which seems pertinent at this juncture is that we ran three theatres, staged some 25 productions a year and had a resident company of never less than 20 and sometimes of over 50 actors.

That was only 11 years ago.

Who the primarily-responsible party is I neither know nor care but the Arts Council of Great Britain, Bristol City Council and Avon County Council have been playing a game of political football with the oldest and most illustrious regional theatre in the country and between them have brought it to the edge of ruin.

Although the ratepayers of Bristol and Avon have every right to be outraged at the continual sapping of the resources that enabled the BOV to be the leading theatre of the region, this disaster is not of merely local importance.

Britain needs regional "centres of excellence" – whatever happened to that idea, by the by? Swept away in the floods of Thatcherite philistinism, I suppose – if the artistic life of the nation is not to devolve entirely around London thus giving 85 per cent of the taxpayers a raw deal.

And there is more to it, too, than the need for an equitable division of the nation's artistic cake: it is in the regional theatres that the seeds of future greatness, which will benefit the whole country and the entire entertainment industry, are sown.

When I was director of the BOV, I did not resent the hours devoted to moneygrubbing and politicking, to all the time spent away from my actors and from the business of directing plays, for that money-grubbing and politicking enabled me, as it enabled my predecessors, to offer talent, when I thought I saw it, a place to grow. To watch an actor at work and be able to think "yes, we'll do 'Hamlet' for him next season" or "it's time she had a stab at 'Hedda' " is what I gladly moneygrubbed and politicked for and would again. Without that possibility, running a theatre becomes only another branch of politics and politics was described by Bernard Shaw as merely "a mug's game."

The choice is as it's always been: do the local authorities and the central funding body want this theatre to be one of the major theatres

of the country or would they rather a battery farm for potboilers? Certainly the Bristol Labour councillor who can announce cretinously "My party is in favour of the arts and also of plays and music" wouldn't know the difference.

As all parties struggle or crawl towards a solution, a deadly trap lies in wait – deadly because it will produce deadly theatre – and that is to accept subsidies of a nature that will leave us, willy nilly, with the battery farm for potboilers. And then the subsidising bodies will sit back with a sigh of relief and say "You see, they didn't really need all that money they said they did anyway."

But the battery farm for potboilers won't produce plays of the calibre to encourage the growth of an Adrian Noble or stretch the talent of a Daniel Day-Lewis; the battery farm for potboilers won't lure actors like Michael Hordern, Daniel Massey, Prunella Scales, Simon Callow, Jane Lapotaire, Julie Walters, Martin Shaw, Lindsay Duncan, Barbara Leigh-Hunt or Richard Pasco to spend time in Bristol; we won't see Tom Stoppard or David Edgar or Peter Nichols in the audience because the battery farm for potboilers won't be doing their plays; the revived Theatre Royal at Bath offers its Bristolian colleague strong and invigorating competition: the battery farm for potboilers won't be able to live up to it.

And the audiences will get smaller and the seats a little dusty and the lights a little dimmer and the ghosts whom Maria Aitken and I encountered when we were rehearsing late one night in the Theatre Royal will no longer walk.

Whenever I was tired or depressed and working late in the theatre, I would go, on my way to the stage door, and sit, all alone, in the dark of the Theatre Royal auditorium. And there the spirits of the actors who have lived and died on that stage eight times a week for over 200 years and the spirits of the audiences who have laughed and wept and applauded their work would form a kind of electrical charge so that I could feel the auditorium tingling. And some of that would pass to me and I would leave the theatre stronger and surer.

Of course, this will seem sentimental rubbish to anyone who hasn't worked in that extraordinary environment. But any actor who's played on that stage or any theatre worker who's sat in that auditorium for long enough to hear its voice will know exactly what I mean. And will, I pray, join me in urging our successors not to accept what will enable mere survival or bare subsistence but to spit in the bastards' eyes and hold out for the cost of excellence!

And I have told an anecdote and given a memory of my time at Bristol, after all.

PAUL DARROW

Other than its London namesake, there is no theatre in the country better known or loved than Bristol's Old Vic and the prospect of acting with this illustrious company fills every actor and actress with a pride and a joy that is not reserved for anywhere else.

When I first set foot on the stage of the Theatre Royal it was with Paul Eddington, Babara Leigh-Hunt and Kate Nelligan and we were to be directed by John Fernald, the former and famous Principal of the Royal Academy of Dramatic Art, in Sir Noel Coward's "Private Lives". Frankly, I was the only one I'd never heard of.

Later I was to work with Charlotte Cornwall, Diana Quick, John Nettles and many more famous names, as well as be directed by Howard Davies.

Now, this famous institution is in danger and that means that we are all in danger. If the Bristol Old Vic falls, then we all fall. "Oh, what a fall would be there, my countrymen. Then you and I and all of us fall down."

So, it won't happen. The Bristol Old Vic, a famous theatre company in a famous city, will survive to flourish again.

If the worst should, uncomprehensibly, be allowed to happen, think of the many ghosts of actors past and present who would haunt King Street. Not only Sarah Siddons would gain revenge.

The Bristol Old Vic offers, indisputably, the best theatre in the land. It is an offer none of us can refuse. For any young actor, and for some who are not so young, Bristol is the most exciting city in Britain. Its buildings are, generally speaking, a pleasure to look at, it has fine restaurants, the best wine merchants, a famous university, an equally famous drama school, a beautiful Theatre Royal and the best and most applauded theatre company outside the West End or Broadway. I know, I've been there.

I was there in the seventies when, if you announced yourself as a member of the Bristol Old Vic Company, people would smile with pleasure and nod with respect. You could perform any part you care to name but, if you performed it in Bristol, you had better be good.

I was in Howard Davies' first production of "Long Day's Journey Into Night", with Paul Eddington, Margaret Ashcroft and Kenneth Cranham. I played the alocholic, schizophrenic older brother. Everyone said I was perfect casting. What was perfect was that we were performing in what is generally regarded as the best theatre in Britain with the best company of actors it was possible to assemble.

Consequently, every actor or actress takes great pride in being able to say, "Oh yes, I was with the Bristol Old Vic." It is the first "credit" we list in the programme of our accomplishments.

Because being a part of the Old Vic's history is so important to every actor, the Theatre Royal lingers like a shadow in our minds and, when we die, we'll come back to haunt the place. Benevolently, of course.

What was that whisper you heard? It was the ghost of an actor sighing with pleasure because he's back at the Old Vic. If you can smell something, it isn't me, it's Sarah Siddons.

Alan Dobie, Eleanor Drew and John Warner in the smash hit "Salad Days", 1954; on transfer, the Reynolds-Slade musical ran for six years at London's Vaudeville Theatre.

More memorable theatre from the 1950s: Barry Wilsher, Wendy Williams and Peter O'Toole in John Osborne's "Look Back in Anger", 1957.

41

PAUL EDDINGTON

The first long run of a play that I ever did was of "A Severed Head", adapted by J. B. Priestley from the novel by Iris Murdoch.

The adventure began, like so many, at the Theatre Royal, King Street, in 1961.

One evening after rehearsal, some of us were having supper in Marco's in the Market. "Do you think it will run?" said Sheila Burrell. "I hope so, dear", replied Heather Chasen, "we've come a long way to do it!"

Eighteen months later, as I sat next to Heather on our way to open the play on Broadway, the pilot told us that we were now 38,000 feet above Bristol. I reminded her of our conversation that night.

The Val May production of "The Taming of the Shrew", 1958/9.

JOHN ELVERY

The lasting memories from 14 years at the Bristol Old Vic are, of course, of the people and of the work. Never did we have enough staff or time to ease the pressure of working very long hours in semi-controlled panic, and the stranger attitudes to the work surface first.

One assistant I had in the design department for a season had a serious problem getting up in the morning. A 2pm arrival at work was considered good after a while, but four or five in the afternoon was quite usual!

The quirks of the audiences too were memorable. The outraged reaction to "Afore Night Come" caught us all by surprise, as it was a well-written play, firmly in the "melodrama" tradition and very well performed and directed; yet it had members of the audience demanding their money back by the interval, long before the play's gruesome ritual-murder which might, certainly, have turned a few stomachs.

An endearing memory is of the company's oldest "fan", 75-years-old at least, being met on the Studio stage by the actors of "Titus Andronicus" returning to start the second half; emerging on hands and knees from a culvert in the stage-setting that she had been exploring during the interval.

My work requiring a close collaboration with the directors, many recollections concern them: from the director who knew just what small stimulus to give me to spark off my imagination in the right direction, to the "dictatorial" approach where one director, wondering what effect a different tie colour would make on a costume design, demanded a complete new painting of the whole design incorporating the different tie colour (several hours' work) so that he could compare the two. Another director, at the very first meeting for a Chekhov play, presented me with a set of ground plans and sketches of the setting he had done, and told me he wanted it to look just like that!

The other extreme was exemplified by the director with whom I had been discussing the designing of a Shakespeare tragedy for months – throwing idea after idea to her and getting absolutely nothing back – at last coming up with the only idea of her own, which, by the way she confided it to me, she obviously thought would inspire me to great design heights.

"Ponder this", she said, "Suppose they all wore "T" shirts with their names on them!"

CHRISTOPHER ETTRIDGE

I was in the company for the first two plays of the 1986 season. The second play was "Talk of The Devil" by Mary O'Malley. It was directed by the then freelance director, Paul Unwin. The production was one of that strange breed that was destined for the West End – but which for various reasons never quite made it.

I played an assortment of religious figures – a parish priest, a bishop and a couple of saints, among whose number was St. Anthony. Paul had given me a sensational entrance in this role. I arose wearing a monk's habit, a beatific smile and a battery-operated halo, on a lift through a trap in the floor – into a 1950s living room and carrying a pair of women's shoes. I swear, it made sense in the plot – but nevertheless the effect was quite bizarre and always got a very good laugh.

The lift on which I arose in saintly state was manually operated from under the stage by a member of crew who shall remain nameless. He would plug in my halo to my battery pack, then on the first cue light he would open the trap and on the second he would haul me up; the magic of theatre . . . except one night, M****** H***** wasn't there. I managed to plug myself in – and then as I could hear my cue starting to get closer, I started to fret. I had already left it too late to

dash upstairs and make a more mundane entrance through the wings
– but I knew I had to get on otherwise the actresses already on stage
would have been seriously in the lurch. The light went on to open the
trap; I unbolted it. If M came now, we would just be OK. He didn't.
Green. There was only one thing for it; halo flashing, habit tangling
my legs, I reached above my head and hauled myself bodily up
through the hole. The audience throught it was tremendous. I got a
round – which made me very happy to forgive M who had been
chatting in the green room and not heard his call . . . in fact, such is
the power of audience approval over some actors, M and I seriously
talked about keeping it in. Unwin vetoed; something about . . .
integrity – which I didn't follow. I swear to this day that if we'd kept
it in we'd have gone to the West End . . . I believe Paul has a different
theory.

The Bristol Old Vic is the only theatre at which I have worked
where the presence of the Christian Church makes a very tangible
presence – in the form of the wonderfully enthusiastic and charm-
ingly stage-struck theatre chaplain, Neville Boundy – known to all as
Nev the Rev. If anyone were to sway me from my firmly-entrenched
atheism, it would surely be someone like Nev.

Each year, the local churches give a tea party for the companies at
the BOV and the Hippodrome. It is always a wonderful spread at
which a great deal of very serious face-stuffing goes on – and from my
experience, very little talk of anything on a higher plane. In 1986 the
party was held in the BOV upstairs bar between the weekday matinée
and evening show of "Talk of The Devil."

In my incarnation as a catholic bishop in the play, I had the most
splendid costume – gold and white cope, mitre – the whole business.
I thought I would see if I could throw the normally imperturbable
Nev by appearing at the party dressed as the bishop. I timed my
entrance well; the party was in full swing; actors were busily servicing
full mouths and full plates; the good church people looked on slightly
bemused. How could so much food disappear down so few people so
sickeningly fast? I approached Nev the Rev; his back was to me; I
tapped him on the shoulder; he turned from the man he was talking
to, looked me up and down – and laughed like a drain. Then without
batting an eyelid, he introduced me to the soberly-besuited man in a
dog collar to whom he had been talking.

"Your Grace," he said to me, "may I introduce you to His Grace,
The Bishop of Bristol." And he walked away and left me.

I have to say I think that round went to the Christians.

ROSEMARY FINNEGAN

I joined the Bristol Old Vic as a trainee theatre manager at the tender age of twenty-two. My training was almost completed within a few months and for the first time I was to be left on my own, in charge of the building, the public and the play in the New Vic Studio. I felt confident and in control, ignoring the theatre manager's emergency telephone numbers should I need any help.

The first half of the evening ran without a hitch, but as I heard the applause at the end of Act 1 I realised I had forgotten to get out the ice-creams. I dashed from my office, down two flights of stairs to the ice-cream room, hastily made up a tray and made my way back again.

In my rush, I slipped on a polished floor wearing high heels. The tray of ice-creams went flying into the air along with my legs and I landed on my right wrist, heard a crack and felt paralysed with pain, I had obviously broken my wrist.

A member of the audience who was looking for the loos spotted me, half-covered in dripping ice-cream, sprawled out in a very unlady-like manner. He came to my rescue and of course asked, "Where can I find the manager?" I smiled weakly and replied, "I am the manager".

With his assistance I made it back to my office and very reluctantly phoned the theatre manager to ask him to return to work. When I had put the telephone down a member of staff came rushing into the office saying "Phone an ambulance" I replied, "I'm not that bad, I'll get a taxi." "Not for you," she said and was followed in by a teenage girl from the audience who had walked into a mirror and had cut her shoulder badly and was bleeding profusely. The girl's friend was in tow and asked "Who's your First Aider?" I thought for about two seconds, nursing my broken wrist and replied "I am." We shared the taxi to the local hospital.

Despite my first night disasters, I remain a member of the Bristol Old Vic staff, enjoying every minute, including the mishaps!

BARRY FOSTER

I've played only twice at the Theatre Royal. Both occasions are intensely memorable: for the spirit of the place itself and for the brilliance of the plays.

In 1960 I was there playing the English soldier in Brendan Behan's wild celebration of Dublin, "The Hostage". Among the cast were

Len Rossiter, Annie Crosbie, Peter Bowles, Ewan Hooper and Frank Middlemass.

In 1979 it was Peter Nichols' great and glorious celebration of his own Bristol, "Born in the Gardens", a four-hander with Beryl Reid, Jennie Linden, again Peter Bowles and directed by the author.

Though vastly different, of course, these two widely-separated productions had at least two things in common: lots of music and the delightful incongruity of projecting noisy, modern riot into this stately, elegant 18th century space. Every evening I walked along King Street to join a seemingly endless, hilarious party given in the Hall of a Great and Gracious Lady who nevertheless continued to smile upon us.

What with that, what with the city and the water itself; with Marco's on the Market steps (actors' lunch 5/- (25p) in 1960); with Clifton, its crescents, pubs, its gorge and bridge; what with the Avon Cities' Jazz Band – there were great times. Great times.

Barry Foster.

JULIAN GLOVER

The second time I played the BOV was in John David's wonderful 1970 production of "Macbeth", with Barbara Leigh-Hunt as Lady Macbeth – who is still, for me, the best I've ever seen. Also in the cast were Jeremy Irons as Seton, Simon Cadell and Tim Pigott-Smith, as a soldier. A not indifferent support group who would verify the following.

Matinées were a great responsibility, as, so often with Shakespeare, they were attended in large numbers by school parties, whose attention we usually managed to hold. One Wednesday afternoon however, we certainly did not. The circle was completely filled by two groups in the 13–15 year-old bracket and of opposing sexes. I mean opposing. They seemed to find the combined elements of being free of school and in proximity to the other sex too powerful to resist; hence a generally negative attitude to what was happening on the stage and a fierce concentration on each other, expressed in terms of paper darts, crisp packets, paper cups, bits of bread and vocal representation of their feelings for each other, plus heavily articulated comments on details of the production which would haphazardly catch their attention. (e.g. woman in nightdress! HOOT!)

It was hell, frankly! But we soldiered on trying to remember that those seated in the stalls were as distracted as us, and wanted to experience the play. I restrained myself, but with difficulty. Until my solo curtain call, when I pointed at the circle to separate clearly its occupants from those below and gave it the biggest floor-to-ceiling V-sign my six-feet-two-inches could manage.

The best laugh of my career, and the applause still rings in my ears! Poor Douglas (Morris) was furious, quite understandably, and, I heard later, vowed never to let me play the Vic again. That vow seemed to work!

All that having been said, the two plays I did in the Theatre Royal remain my two happiest theatrical memories and I can only hope the audiences shared some of my joy in them. It would be too awful if future generations were to be denied the experience of the Bristol Old Vic.

50

EDWARD HARDWICKE

I spent the first three years of my acting life at the Bristol Old Vic and they remain the happiest I have enjoyed as an actor.

We often used to eat at Marco's, an Italian restaurant near the theatre. In those days Italian restaurants were rare and very special. Even so, on a weekday the set lunch was 2/3d (12.5 pence today). But the real treat was lunch on a Saturday, more expensive, and only an à la carte menu. Marco was always at the till when we paid our bill and the girls were always given a rose. No matter what we'd spent he would charge us 2/3d. Later, whenever I was near Bristol, I always went to Marco's and took friends. He knew how to run a restaurant.

About that time the company developed a dangerous tendency towards elaborate jokes on stage. Any new member could receive the treatment. It was a great honour and meant you had arrived. On one occasion, however, the tables were turned.

An actor joined the company who appeared to have no sense of humour whatsoever. Far too serious for our tastes, arrogant and aloof, he had a long lugubrious face, which never smiled. He arrived to be in a play called "The Lamp at Midnight", about Galileo. During rehearsals the play became increasingly unpopular, endless short scenes with thirty or more characters, this meant a great deal of doubling and changing hats. Always dangerous when laughter is near.

Once running, the on-stage jokes in this production increased to almost epidemic proportions. Never in the presence of our new company member, possibly the author's spy. The climax of the first act was a scene in which this particular actor, playing the president of a science society, addressed its members, who were considering electing Galileo to their number. It was one of the longer scenes and the entire company was on stage.

I remember that it finished with an impassioned plea to elect Galileo, interrupted by the angelus ringing and everyone falling to their knees in prayer: curtain. His speech began: "Thirteen years ago today, we formed this Society of the Lynx. That was our first step towards liberating the sciences in our country . . ." It was a long speech and continued for two or three minutes.

Not at this performance. He rose to his feet: "Thirteen years ago today, we formed this Society of the Lynx. That was out first big mistake."

He then sat down. You can imagine the effect on the rest of the cast. There was hardly a dry anything on stage. How we finished the act I will never know.

He later told me that to prevent breaking down himself he needed days of serious and humourless behaviour to carry out his act of anarchy. He was immediately elected president of our club. I hasten to add that we did do some memorable productions that season and we all behaved impeccably!

It was a joyous time, and it is sad that young actors and actresses today so rarely have the opportunity to enjoy that kind of life in theatre; the fun, the camaraderie, and the hard work, in a company like the Bristol Old Vic.

Edward Hardwicke

CHRIS HARRIS

This seems crazy, it's Bastille Day and I'm in West Africa where I am directing the National Theatre of Namibia in a production of "The Playboy of the Western World", retitled "The Playboy of West Africa." It seems incongruous to be sitting in this newly-independent democracy thinking of the Bristol Old Vic, although I did play the title role there in '69. However, as I think, I smile. For 23 years now I have been committed to "The Gaff" – I spread its word wherever I go and I still regard it to be my spiritual home.

Here are some snapshots of that glorious association like . . .

– running between the Little and the Theatre Royal to be in both productions. I believe someone was actually in all three venues.
– taking Val May to see the girl change into a gorilla at Lai Chi Kok on BOV's visit to the Hong Kong Festival '72.
– like listening to Jeremy Irons tuning his guitar for "The Servant of Two Masters". He bought my VW Beetle the next day.
– like laughing until we had laundry problems as Conni Chapman, playing Mrs. Leverett in "Rookery Nook", passed out behind the sofa . . . She was, dear reader, OK!
– like the absolute joy of John David and Tony Staveacres' "Fred Karno's Army". Why did that not go on to London?
– like the Christmas parties and Fred Stacey's Punk Band.
– like the costume fittings with Harry Reader and his girls in those tunnels of excitement beneath the Colston Hall.
– like directing "Dick Whittington" in the New Vic and creating the transformation with a huge inflatable.
– like standing on stage with Dame Sybil on the closing of the Old Vic for redevelopment in 1970.
– like West Country tours with Thelma Barlow, Marcia Warren & co.

I have to finish there as it's time to go back to rehearsals. Would that it were at BOV.

Felicity Kendal and Michael Hordern in "Once Upon a Time", March, 1976.

LOUISE JAMESON

"Some memory of your time at Bristol Old Vic." This was the request. They literally pour through my mind.

Two brief but very joyous affairs with my leading men, an horrific chase through Clifton at two in the morning by the man known as the Bristol Rapist; meeting an extraordinary woman, a probation officer, who introduced me to "Dirty Den" then in prison; playing Portia in a surgical corset supporting my slipped disc and having the wonderful Richard Cottrell waiting in the wings, his arms open, hugging me, turning me round, pushing me back on stage; wearing stolen daffodils in my hair en route to rehearsal; working with John Dove, without doubt the best director I have come across in 20 years; Harold Innocent making me wet myself with laughter one night, locked out of his and everyone else's digs – and refusing to come back and share mine; discovering I was pregnant with my second child and having to do Restoration Comedy *without* my corset!

Bristol has always represented life-changing cross roads for me, however the story I choose to tell is more humbling than momentous.

Louise Jameson (centre) as Helena with John Telfer (Lysander) and Caroline Holdaway (Hermia) in "A Midsummer Night's Dream", Summer 1980.

It was a balmy, barmy first night party, "A Midsummer Night's Dream". Imaginatively directed by Richard Cottrell, exquisitely designed by Bob Crowley. The scene is set in Renato's, the Renato's opposite the theatre, crammed in – all of us, and a few partners and supporters. Secure in the knowledge of our success (we later transferred to the Old Vic by Waterloo), heady on applause and wine, someone . . . who was it? had a guitar. By this time the audience-inhabited tables were deserted – bored by the noise, fed-up of the zoo-spectacle of pissed actors, or just plain tired, they'd gone home. We let rip. As always no hassle from Mr. & Mrs. Renato – in fact I believe champagne flowed freely and for free (How he ever makes a profit is beyond me). Mrs. R. came out of the kitchen and Renato said in passing, what a good voice she had. Well, we forced her to sing. Standing shyly in the corner a tea towel in her hand. The room stilled, she started . . . her talent was breath-taking – an aria from I don't know where – Heaven I think – filled the room. We stopped congratulating ourselves and watched her, enthralled. She finished, a moment's pause and then we're screaming for more. On our feet, stamping, whistling. She shakes her head and, blushing, runs from the room.

It was wonderful. Like picking spinach as the sun sets in my garden, a spiritually humbling moment. A glorious celebration of another talent, another culture, another time.

Jane Lapotaire with Constance Chapman on the left in the 23rd season production of "The Way of the World".

JANE LAPOTAIRE

This is really not my story at all, it was told to me by Paul Eddington, but as he was a stalwart member of the Bristol Old Vic Theatre Company, I feel I am justified in sneaking it as my own – hoping, of course, he hasn't contributed the same.

During the 50s Paul was involved in the filming of Richard Greene's "Robin Hood of Sherwood Forest". They used to be made up and costumed in the television studios and then transferred to location in a 'bus and returned from filming in the same way i.e. in full slap and Lincoln green.

On one particular occasion the 'bus was held up in a long stream of traffic and, much to the actors' consternation, they realised that the jam had been caused by an accident to some cars ahead of them. Not remembering that they were in full Sherwood Forest disguise – but being generous and helpful of spirit as most actors are! – they leapt out of the 'bus and ran to the head of the traffic queue to see what was happening.

Well, you can imagine the reaction on the faces of the poor people involved in what thankfully turned out to be only a minor bump as, dazed with shock and rather bewildered, they opened their eyes to be confronted by Little John, Friar Tuck and Robin Hood. They must have thought that they had gone to some peculiar kind of heaven!

BARBARA LEIGH-HUNT

The Bristol Old Vic – oh, how I wish I could convey the excitement and tremendous sense of anticipation those words engendered in me as a girl in my early 'teens, still at school but no scholar and hell-bent on a career in the theatre.

I did not come from a "privileged" background by any means. My mother had left my father and was bringing me up on her own with no financial help – no income support or child allowances in those days – so, to support us, she worked for Boots the Chemist. Six days a week, first as an ordinary counter assistant and then as head of department. Money was very short, but somehow, bless her, she managed to take me every week to the Theatre Royal in Bath and occasionally – very occasionally as a special treat, to the Bristol Old Vic.

And what joys awaited us there – such productions – "A Penny for a Song" by John Whiting, "Family Reunion" and "Venus Observ'd" by T. S. Eliot, "The Duenna" by Sheridan, "The River Line" by Charles Morgan, "Macbeth", "Hamlet" with the young pre-nose job O'Toole, "Two Gentlemen of Verona" and many more. The actors too, Peter O'Toole, John Neville, Laurence Payne – I can hear to this day his reading of "On, the uncertain glory of an April day . . ." – Alan Dobie, Douglas Campbell, Norman Rossington, Bob Harris, James Cairncross, Robert Cartland, Beatrix Lehmann, Pamela Allen, Jane Wenham, Dorothy Reynolds, Pauline Jameson – as well as the directors and designers who shaped this journey for the imagination. Because this is what it was – an unparalleled introduction to dramatic literature and professional theatre.

Later, of course, I became a student at the Bristol Old Vic Theatre School and subsequently had the honour and delight of acting in the company at the Theatre Royal and at the Little Theatre, of helping to carry the name of the BOV with tours in this country and abroad, and last, but by no means least in my list of priorities, one of the most important factors in my life, for which again I have to thank this wonderful old theatre and its company – I met my husband-to-be while I was in its employ!

But the BOV has had an enduring effect on many people's lives – I am constantly surprised and delighted by the people I meet who say, "I saw you many times at the Theatre Royal when I was a student." They usually go on to say how much those visits to the theatre meant, how they enriched their lives when they were young men and women of slender means.

A great city like Bristol has a rare "jewel in its crown" in the Bristol Old Vic's Theatre Royal. The work of this theatre and its company has an important contribution to make – a "platform" where the playwrights of the past, present and future can speak to us of man's condition down the ages and show us with what resource, talent, wisdom, wit and no little humour, he copes with his practical and spiritual problems – and, simply to entertain us when the going gets tough!

Barbara Leigh-Hunt in "Blithe Spirit", 1966.

58

PIP MAYO

On the whole, I think practical jokes are tiresome, but I greatly enjoyed the trick we played on Chris Harris and "The Bristol Twins" company during Christmas 1980.

I was playing one of Beauty's silly sisters in "Beauty and the Beast", in the Studio. Our show came down earlier than "The Bristol Twins" in the main house, and just at the point when they had a big chase scene. During the final performance (with no possibility of a come-back) the Theatre Royal audience were witness to the entire cast of "Beauty and the Beast" (Julia Hills, Peter Woodward, Jenny Galloway, David Stoll, Patrick Malahide, Susannah Morley and myself), all still in full costume as Beast, Wizard, Dragon and human characters, rushing across the stage as an unrehearsed addition to the chase.

The audience loved it and Chris Harris – a true pro – was completely taken aback – for the briefest of seconds.

ADRIAN NOBLE

I won an award from the Regional Theatre Trainee Directors' Scheme to join the Bristol Old Vic for a period of two years beginning in 1976. Richard Cottrell was the incumbent artistic director and his policy was classical; the repertoire should centre around works drawn from the great English tradition of playwriting from the Elizabethans through the Jacobeans, Restoration, Farquhar, Sheridan, Shaw – the backbone rep of most theatres up and down the country since the Second World War. But he went beyond most theatres in his ambitions. He wanted to create a true company, an ensemble of actors and directors and designers who would together create a body of work in Bristol that could equal the very best in the land.

And I think in large measure he succeeded. If you compare the cast lists and associate list of the Bristol Old Vic in the late seventies with that of say the Royal Shakespeare Company in the mid-eighties you will find a large number of names common to each. Richard's great unsung talent was to collect together extraordinary groups of people just at the moment before they became nationally and sometimes internationally famous; this he did spectacularly with the Actors Company and then, just as importantly, at the Bristol Old Vic in the late seventies.

For us who were a part of it, it was indeed a golden time, and looking back it was probably part of a golden time in the repertory theatre around the country. I myself in one year directed a play by Shakespeare, a Jacobean tragedy, a play by Brecht and a pantomime. I worked in three different spaces equally challenging. It was the theatre in which I learnt not only my craft but the appreciation of a set of values that have lived with me up until today, and stay with me in my present job at the head of the Royal Shakespeare Company.

The gap between the opportunities we were given a short twelve years ago and the appalling plight the Bristol Old Vic now finds itself in speaks for itself. You could argue that a town gets the kind of theatre it deserves and to a degree this is, of course, true. But a theatre company is a living organism, an intricate, interrelated set of ideas and personalities which requires a measure of stability and security to flourish properly.

I would say to the local Bristol politicians, "On behalf of the citizens of Bristol you have a custodial role over the arts in your area. The Bristol Old Vic is not yours to run down or to squander; you've borrowed it for a short period of time and I would argue your responsibility is to pass it on to future generations in a better artistic and financial state than the one in which you received it".

Excuse my cheek.

Adrian Noble

RICHARD PASCO

In the late 'fifties and early 'sixties my career had got into that state of frequent unemployment which comes to all actors; of waiting between, at best, a play in the "West End" (there had been one or two of these which had run six weeks, eight weeks, three months even and had sunk without trace, never to be revived) interspersed with a "one-off" television play, very studio-bound and studio set. Perhaps if one was lucky, there would be a more stimulating play for radio and at the time I write about, being extremely lucky, working on a Hammer-horror film. But there was no significant challenge to make it all seem worthwhile after years of "rep" and classical training. Working on the aforementioned film I was one day summoned to the telephone, a voice said, "Val May here, will you come down to Bristol and lead our Shakespeare quatercentenary celebrations by playing "Henry V" and Berowne in "Love's Labour's Lost" with a tour abroad after the season in Bristol?" I did not hesitate and so my very first visit to the Theatre Royal in King Street began.

The Oxford Companion to the Theatre says: *Bristol*: Home of the Bristol Old Vic and of the first university in England to have a drama department." The beauty of that auditorium when I first walked into it made me pause for breath, this magical old working theatre, then undisturbed by "development"; and my dreams of working in such a place about to be fulfilled.

What did Bristol Old Vic mean to an actor in his late thirties in the midst of the so-called "Swinging Sixties"? Elitist? I really was not aware of the word used as a term of ridicule as it is today; a theatre for the dull "middle-class" etc. etc. The theatre played to 90% capacity in plays covering the classics, revivals and new work (a lot of which became highly successful in the commercial theatre). The audience was a vibrant cross-section of Bristolians young and old and a fair sprinkling of visitors from abroad, drawn to the magic of the Old Vic Company, the only theatre to retain that title in those days.

Its patron, certainly, was HRH Princess Marina of Kent, who gave not only her name but her presence to several productions and her blessing on our Shakespeare efforts before setting off on the arduous nine-months tour of Europe and Israel which followed on from the season in Bristol itself. Miss Jennie Lee (Aneurin Bevan's widow), perhaps the most enlightened and generous Minister for the Arts this country has ever known, was a frequent visitor and warm supporter of all the efforts of management, staff, crew and actors under the hallowed old roof.

Tradition? Certainly (another dirty word these days but for the life of me I cannot understand why). What is wrong with the past glories encapsulated in that word, when it embraces Mrs. Siddons, Macready, Irving, Kean, Ellen Terry, all of whom had trodden those worn old boards (where are those old boards and stage machinery now?).

Val May's invitation to me meant the chance to join and help create an ensemble company that would work and stay together through the extremes of travel abroad in all kinds of auditoria, the maintenance of performance standards, and, to use another un-popular word, by good old theatre discipline. And so it was. The response to Stuart Burge's production of "Henry V" and Val May's "Love's Labour's Lost" was unanimous and the company that I was proud to lead was rapturously received from King Street to Frankfurt, Brussels to Copenhagen, Oslo to Helsinki. Equally to Israel, which was re-visited in 1967 on the second major world tour that stemmed from the Theatre Royal, to the USA and Canada. Return dates to Europe too of Val May's productions of "Hamlet", "Romeo and Juliet" and no less than the great Tyrone Guthrie's production of "Measure for Measure". Guthrie had chosen to work at Bristol in preference to other probably more lucrative offers because at that time the name Bristol Old Vic was a big attraction in itself.

The changing face of BOV programmes.

There is already now a healthy interchange of productions between Bristol and the Royal National Theatre and this must be built on and the theatre once again elevated to its former prominence in English theatre. My four years' connection directly or indirectly with Bristol, and one return visit in the 'seventies to work with the excellent Richard Cottrell, are milestones in my memory, years to set by my work with the RSC and the NT. Perhaps without the years in Bristol I would never have been accepted by these eminent leading companies.

So this playhouse must stay, expand and embrace all who, in the future, will hope to pass into that golden auditorium as members of a thriving audience; and the future generations of actors and actresses will enter the stage door and appear in front of that continuing audience, who in the past heard the voices of the hallowed names that those of us who love the Theatre will respect and remember to the end of our days.

Richard Pasco.

TIM PIGOTT-SMITH

Leaving school in 1964 to come to Bristol to study drama represented for me the beginnings of realising a dream. To walk through the stage door of the Theatre Royal as an employee in August 1969, after three years at Bristol University and two years at Bristol Old Vic Theatre school, was the dream come true.

To be involved in theatre in any way in the '60s was exciting: things seemed possible. How different now. How hard it is for us to imagine the idealistic fervour with which we were going to take drama into everybody's lives and show them the life-enhancing potential of the theatre. How many students will leave the BOVTS this year and go straight into a ten-month job at the Theatre Royal? – there were six of us in '69. Drama, theatre itself it seems, is now fighting for its life; and Mrs. Thatcher has the naive audacity to tell us that the arts are flourishing. We do more, on less money, and have to fight harder and harder to be able to make the next step. Is there a lesson that can be learnt from drama to sustain us in these straitened times?

If the great plays of our past teach us anything, they celebrate the triumph of the spirit in adversity and the potential for rebirth when things seem at their worst. I played Amiens and Charles the wrestler in "As You Like It" in 1970 at Bristol – the last production in the old theatre before the present refurbishments were made.

Revisiting the theatre to see work in progress, I was shocked to see the vulnerable shell of the stage area – standing small amidst the rubble – waiting for the new buildings to surround and protect it. A sheet of corrugated iron filled the proscenium arch. Here stood the "acting area", and it looked wretched; yet never have I been so acutely aware of ghosts – the ghosts of all the performances that had filled that space over two hundred years – not just Mrs. Siddons and the old man who used to pop in during rehearsals, but the ghosts of my own short time at the theatre.

It was an excitement and a relief to come back later to the re-opening and it has been good to see the new buildings acquire ghosts of their own over the last twenty years.

The Bristol Old Vic is vulnerable now in a way it has never been, but I believe the efforts and concern of those who care for it, and who promote the value of a community enriched by culture will prevail. They must. They will.

As I write I am just about to play Salieri in Peter Shaffer's great play "Amadeus": he reminds the audience that the "savour" of life in the 1780s remains behind because of the music of the period . . . "our music still remembered, whilst their politics is long forgotten . . ."

Tim Rgsl. Smith

DONALD PLEASENCE

Sir Newton Blick was a great actor and a great friend. His title was honorary, given to him by the cast of 1949–50 (Pamela Allan, Gudron Ure, Donald Sinden, John Neville, Stuart Burge, Donald Pleasence, Hugh Manning *et al*). This honour was given to him for his services to the theatre, to humanity and to the Old Duke, Bristol where he drank every night after the show.

We thought up a special prize for a drama school. It would be given to the student who could remove the padding, whiskers and costume

of Falstaff and be half way through his first pint in the nearest pub five minutes after the curtain fell.

I dressed with him and I saw this feat accomplished at least a dozen times during the run of "The Merry Wives of Windsor". He never spoke during the removal of make-up and costume. Padding came off silently, whiskers, wig, clothes. All put away, all tidy. I marvelled at that; my own clothes were strewn across the room. Newton's were hung up, even his wig, pinned neatly to the wig block. Yet he was out of the dressing room in three minutes and into the pub in four. I never beat him. By the time I got into the Duke he would be halfway through a pint of Guinness.

I was abroad when he died. Denis Carey told me that, after drinking several pints of Guinness, he left a pub in Dublin and died instantly outside. He was buried in Ireland. Newton Blick was loved by all who knew him and it is to his memory that these few lines are dedicated.

AMANDA REDMAN

I left the Bristol Old Vic Theatre School thirteen years ago and was extremely fortunate to be asked to join the Bristol Old Vic Company in my last term. I stayed for a year and I can honestly say that I learnt as much about the business in that short time as I have done since!

It was a very exciting period for the Bristol Old Vic as Richard Cottrell was in his hey-day and he filled the three working theatres with some of the bravest productions around – certainly in the provinces. He also employed top-class actors who were willing to come down to Bristol for little pay compared to the National and the RSC but they knew the work would be first rate.

"Cotty" as Richard is affectionately known, is an exacting director but very clever and innovative. His assistant at that time was Adrian Noble who is currently running the RSC. I remember as a student being thrilled by Adrian's directorial debut which he followed up with more stunners including "Titus Andronicus", which had people queueing around the block to get seats.

The actors who were leading in all these productions included such luminaries as Jane Lapotaire, Simon Callow, Barbara Leigh-Hunt, Richard Pasco, Maria Aitken, Julie Walters, John Shrapnell, Prunella Scales and many, many more. I learnt an amazing amount just by watching and supporting them and I suppose the sadness I feel today is that youngsters coming out of drama schools cannot possibly be benefiting from the same sort of experiences as the money is just not there to attract those kind of first-rate actors, nor is it available to fund three shows running concurrently as was the case in my day.

Having said that, the Bristol Old Vic still put on some of the best shows outside of London and the atmosphere surrounding the front of house in King Street continues to be rather lovely. There is a kind of old world charm in the manners of the staff and they always convey the impression that they feel privileged to be working in the oldest and most beautiful theatre in England. Add to all this the incredibly high standards in the various technical departments at Bristol and we have a theatre which I and countless esteemed colleagues would feel proud to work in at any time.

Please don't let it die – the loss to our profession would be phenomenal!

Amanda Redman

Two world premières in 1981: June Barrie, Linsey Beauchamp and Peter Copley in Brian Jefferies' "Beside the Sea', and Joanne Pearce and Christian Rodska in the New Vic production of "The Governess", part of "The Dostoevsky Trilogy".

Junior cast list for "The Adventures of Mr. Toad", 1987/8 in alphabetical order: Kate Anstey, Katy Beazer, Carolyn Cole, Claire Evans, Aviva Epstein, Shelley Hastings, Natasha Leo, Fay McDonald, Lucy McKerron, Louise Mitchell, Jenny Moody, Christopher Mulhearn, Joanna Pollicutt, Kate Redmond, Neville Solomon, Gemma Shortman, Kim Thomas, Mikala Waldron, Joanna Wallace and Kelly Wright.

LEONARD ROSSITER

The late Leonard Rossiter, who became famous for his TV comedies and hilarious TV advertisements, spent early years as an actor at Bristol Old Vic. He recalled those years in an interview in 1983.

I first came to Bristol in 1959 to join the Bristol Old Vic. I'd been an actor for four years then, but I hadn't really got anywhere. I went on doing weekly rep and pantos and in 1958 got a part in a Julian Slade musical in London. That gave me confidence to audition at Bristol which then, as now, had a terrific reputation. John Hale was the artistic director.

Somehow everything went right for those two years. I found my acting feet, got the parts I felt were right for me, did everything from Shakespeare to Shaw – and discovered I had a talent for comedy.

I worked for wonderful directors, the kind of people who later set my career in motion, and it was a wonderful company: it had Peter Bowles, Peter Jeffrey, Annette Crosbie, Newton Blick and Barry Foster in it and we all worked together well.

We are all cricket mad too, we used to play in the street, The Rackhay, outside the stage door. The cobbles had a strange effect on the bowling. I remember we played a journalists' team that had Tom Stoppard in it. He was working for the *Western Daily Press*.

But it wasn't just the theatre that I loved. I loved the whole city as well. I felt at home in Bristol. I used to spend a lot of my spare time sitting on the quay near the theatre watching the boats and learning my lines. It was such a free time. I had no obligations and on the £30 a week that I earned you could live quite well then. I used to eat my lunch at Marco's sometimes, and I remember it cost six shillings (30p). I bet it doesn't now. In a way I suppose my time at Bristol was the equivalent of my university.

My first digs were in St. Michael's Hill: they were a bit grim, and the day I arrived I told the landlord I would like a bath.

"A bath?" he said. "On a Sunday?" So I didn't stay there long.

I moved to a garden flat in Pembroke Road, just by the new Clifton Cathedral.

I took my driving test up on the Downs and before we started the examiner said, "Just read me the number of that blue car over there".

I couldn't even see a blue car, so in a panic, I made a number up.

Leonard Rossiter in "The Clandestine Marriage", Autumn, 1959, with Newton Blick and Ewan Hooper.

He accepted it. He hadn't looked himself! So I passed, and my instructor couldn't believe it!

I learned the Bristol "l" from an electrician at the theatre: he used to talk about the stage areal and Cinderellal. We were very naughty: we did a production of the "Taming of The Shrew" and kept talking about "Padual and Mantual". I was a Dame in the Christmas show and Jessie Matthews played Fairy Filthy Froth!

I used to spend hours on the Suspension Bridge, watching the climbers on the rocks beneath.

Oh, this is a trip down nostalgia lane. I just remember my time here as being one of unrelieved happiness. Now, as you can see, everyone recognises me and says, "Hello Leonard, can I have your autograph?", but back in 1959 I was a total unknown, intent on making a name for myself.

Back on a visit like this, you can't entirely recreate the happiness, or recapture the way it was. But Bristol will always be a special place to me. It was here I grew up as an actor.

A scene from "A Town in the West Country", by Don Hale, October, 1988.

Joely Richardson in "Lady Windermere's Fan", Spring, 1990.

PRUNELLA SCALES

Quite simply I have learned my job at the Bristol Old Vic. In 1952
I was an acting ASM there, fresh out of drama school, being drilled by
the resident stage manager, Michael Ashford (who came to see us on
tour in Cardiff a month or so ago, now retired and much less for-
bidding than I remembered him). I learned to change plugs, give
cues, run the show from the corner and sit on the book at rehearsals,
though I was never very good at cleating flats.

One day the director Denis Carey found me sweeping the stage,
seized the broom from my hand saying "That's not the way to do
it, you mustn't raise the dust", and was puzzled to find that his
admirable and efficient demonstration reduced me to helpless sobs.
I was being less than adequate in all my small acting parts and to be
found inadequate in stage-sweeping was, well, profoundly depressing.
But of course I'm grateful now to have learned about the technical
side at first hand.

I also had my first professional experience as a director at the Vic in the days of John Hale, and my first major leading part in a Russian classic "A Month in the Country", directed by John Dove in 1979. Looking back I realise that every time I have been back to Bristol it has meant the opening of a new door, because the standard there in all departments is so consistently high you can't fail to learn every time you go there.

On "Long Day's Journey Into Night" this year, a co-production with the National Theatre, the heads of department from the South Bank were staggered at the standards of skill and excellence they found at the Bristol Old Vic, particularly perhaps in the wardrobe, which carries one of the few remaining men's tailoring departments in the regions.

I can't bear to think that the future of this priceless centre of creative excellence is threatened for want of a few thousand pounds. What sort of indictment will that be of a nation of alleged theatre lovers?

I also find misinformed the allegations of "elitism" levelled at the BOV from certain quarters: this is a people's theatre, with low seat prices, offering a broad cultural repertoire, accessible to people of all ages and income brackets. If it is to remain so, instead of becoming a mere four-walls, non-producing theatre, offering a bland succession of pre- or post-West End tours, subsidy is necessary. A local theatre should provide a service, first to the whole local population and secondly to the profession at large by the training and experience it offers to the writers, designers, directors, actors and technicians working in it.

The BOV has done this triumphantly over the years: Bristol cannot afford to lose it.

Eve Pearce played the aunt in Lorca's "Dona Rosita", Autumn, 1989.

Adrian Scarborough, Wale Ojo and Jude Akuwudike in Athol Fugard's "Master Harold and the boys", Spring, 1990.

JAMES TALJAARD

It was the first night of a new season. Our production was "A Town In The West Country", a community play involving 120 of the finest amateur performers and the expertise of the BOV stage staff. It was about Bristol during the Blitz. We had King Street completely sealed off for the week, all the offices had taped their windows to make everything look authentic, we had early 1900s cars and even a bomb in it.

At about 6pm, two hours before curtain-up, a member of the box office came into my office. "There's a bomb in King Street," he said.

"I know, we put it there," I replied.

"No I've just received a threat on the phone."

"Oh Gosh", I said or words to that effect.

I telephoned the police and told them we had received a call from a person with an Irish accent saying "There's a bomb in King Street. It will go off at 8pm."

The police asked me what I wanted to do. I said evacuate the building.

By this time the performers were having supper in the buttery, 120 of them. We put the evacuation procedure into force and the entire building was empty in three-and-a-half minutes.

The police arrived and put up red tape at the end of the street. Then the officer in command gave me a choice, "Wait two hours for the Bomb Squad to arrive", (but with the show due to start in 45 minutes' time this did not sound good news), or a selected few could search the premises. After a word with the director, we had no choice. The show had to go on. So five of us entered the building and began to search.

The Studio was clear, so was the Garrick Bar and the stalls. I walked slowly and nervously up the stairs to the Siddons Bar and suddenly I was struck with horror. In my haste to clear the eating area, I had neglected to advise the performers to take their bags with them.

There were 103 bags, holdalls, even a few shoe boxes, under tables, on chairs, in the darker corners. We had no choice but carefully and by now with the assistance of a number of PCs to search every bag.

The eventual start of the performance . . . 8.10pm . . . the same evening.

BOV House Manager, James Taljaard with Deputy House Manager, Rosemary Finnegan.

Dorothy Tutin as Phebe and Emrys Jones as Silvius in the 1950 production of "As You Like It".

DOROTHY TUTIN

O, Bristol and the beautiful Bristol Old Vic!

Immediate memories – being 19, living in digs, in a garret with no hot water overlooking the rooftops – which I adored, and walking down Christmas Steps to the theatre in the snow.

I had been told it was a beautiful theatre but when I stood on the stage for the first time I was so excited and enraptured – it was the first "proper" stage I had worked on and the auditorium, with its perfect proportions and atmosphere, made me think I might be an actress after all . . .

I earned £8 a week and saved £2.

I learned so much on that stage. Most of the company were much older than me, or so it seemed, and they were very clever and brilliant and I would sit in the pubs and cafés feeling I was being educated by listening to them.

I learned that to play a maid and dust busily through someone else's funny lines was not good and I learned several new swear words when the actor involved berated me – loudly.

When I played the boy Lucius in "Julius Caesar", I learned that some of the men in the company suddenly seemed very friendly! But not till the end of the play did I find out that the reason why my walk was rather successfully boyish was because I had two left-footed sandals!

I learned that although I was hardly aware of all the sexual implications in lines as Belinda in "The Provok'd Wife", by copying the leading lady and saying things with innuendo, I got away with it.

I learned that you mustn't get sunburnt when wearing an off-the-shoulder dress as I did in "Tartuffe". Walking around Clifton I became so red I almost had to be whitewashed – it was very painful.

More than anything, I wanted to come back the following season (and play perhaps rather larger parts) instead of walking on and understudying as I had been offered at the Old Vic, London, which my agent thought I ought to accept because they might not ask me again. And it so turned out that the new director of Bristol came to see us all one matinée and for reasons I can't go into here, we all got the giggles at the end of the play. Me particularly. It was agony and awful and none of us were ever invited to join his company.

I didn't come back till "Portrait of a Queen" to play Victoria many years and a baby later. I found the same magic in that theatre, in fact I'm sure that opening there was a major contribution to its success.

Actors and that theatre are "at home" with each other! I wish I were there still.

81

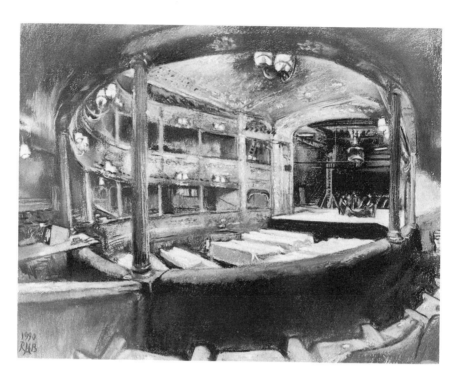

During 1990, Bristol artist Rachel Bray studied, drew and painted the life of the Bristol Old Vic.
Sewing in the wardrobe department, life in the office, the make-up and dressing rooms, backstage
workings and production set-ups for all the year's plays are recorded in some 90 works.
In this picture we see the "set up" for "Lady Windermere's Fan". The chandelier is being raised
into place and yards of green fabric are being arranged as walls for Lord Windermere's study.

JULIE WALTERS

This story was attributed to the Bristol Old Vic while I was there:

There was a production of "Macbeth" on and it was a matinée performance. One actor playing McB started the speech "Tomorrow and tomorrow and tomorrow . . ." when a little old lady in the front row was heard to say "That'll be Wednesday".

Julie Walters with Timothy Kightley in the Autumn, 1978 production of "The Changeling".

RODNEY WEST

It is a trick of memory that when asked to recall a special, or even a random, occasion, one's mind goes instantly and completely blank. When talking to groups about the Theatre Royal, an almost guaranteeable question was, "What is the funniest thing that has ever happened to you?" And, similarly, I could never remember anything which seemed to be remotely amusing, although most of my days in the Theatre were filled with laughter and with incidents more bizarre and ridiculous than anything we ever put on stage.

After twenty two years at the Theatre Royal, there are inevitably many wonderful memories associated with it, and with the remarkable people with whom I worked, and it is almost invidious to choose one rther than any other. The Hong Kong Lift Story is probably my must famous incident, but although this has been retold many times, I still dine out on it and am not yet ready to commit it to print.

When I first joined the Bristol Old Vic, there were several great characters on the staff, most of whom had worked at the Theatre for many years. One of the greatest was our Housekeeper, the wonderful Violet Lane, an absolute natural raconteuse and comedienne, who kept the Theatre Manager's office happily amused for hours on end almost every morning. Violet, and her team of ladies, firmly believed that the ghost of Sarahl Siddons resided in the Theatre Royal, even if they had never actually seen her.

84

Shortly after the Redevelopment (1972) a new cleaner was employed who, Violet reported, was extremely septical (*sic*) about ghosts in general and about the Theatre Royal's in particular. Early one morning the cleaner was working in the Dressing Rooms – spanking new and, one would imagine, as far removed from eighteenth century ghosts as it was possible to be.

As she bent over to clean a dressing table, she felt something lightly brush past her – perhaps someone's cloak, or a large sleeve. She looked up quickly to find out who was with her, but could see nothing, neither in the large looking-glass in front of her, nor as she turned to look back into the room. What she did see was that all the dresses and spare hangers on the wardrobe-rail were swaying gently to and fro, as if a passing shoulder had just clipped them as it went towards the door. The door, however, remained firmly closed – until opened by the cleaner herself as she rushed, screaming, from the room. It took much fanning from the other cleaner's aprons, and a good deal of brandy, to calm her down.

"Well now", announced Violet, as she regaled the office with this story later in the day. "she isn't septical any longer".

TIMOTHY WEST

No, there weren't people with buckets collecting money for the rebuilt Theatre Royal when, in 1972, it opened again to the Bristol public – no fund-raising dinners, no press battles between the management and members of the City Council; just a sense of excited achievement and civic pride. But then things were a lot easier in some ways in 1972.

The show with which Val May chose to exhibit the newly-designed main house stage was "Trelawny", a musical adaptation of Pinero's play by George Rowell, Aubrey Woods and Julian Slade. The plot, dealing as it does with bringing new theatrical ideas into old theatre buildings, could not have been more appropriate to the occasion and the technical staff, presented for the first time with masses of space and some up-to-date equipment, rose accordingly. Patrons may remember Hayley Mills running on the spot while a seemingly-endless street of shops passed across the stage behind her, and an entire fully-dressed Victorian drawing room evaporating piece-meal without any apparent human agency, leaving Ian Richardson finishing his number on a vast empty stage before an enormous blue cyclorama.

Most people were glad to see the end of the cramped old canopied

access in King Street – nothing to do with the original design, a Victorian afterthought – and liked the spacious if austere dignity of the theatre's adopted contemporary, the Coopers' Hall, as the new front-of house area. The choice of heavy brown-patterned wallpaper combined with mauve carpets may I think be open to question, and there are some of us who look forward intensely to the fruition of the current building plan to jolly the place up a bit. But in 1972 people were grateful for the unaccustomed space in which to eat (only basic snacks though in those days), drink and chat about the play.

"Trelawny" was a sell-out, and audiences loved it. We did too, everyone's heart and energy was committed to the production; it was a very happy time. I had to go to Australia immediately the run finished, and while I was there plans were made to bring the show into the West End. I was not able to rejoin the cast, not being due back in England until the day before the opening, but I did actually attend the first night at the Prince of Wales Theatre in London.

I sat there amazed. We seemed to be watching a completely different show. Some of the cast replacements (not mine, I hasten to add; the late Max Adrian was wonderful) appeared to have been chosen to provide an altogether brasher approach to the evening. Julian's charming score (his best, I think), played by a quintet at Bristol, was re-orchestrated for a pit of seventeen at the Prince of Wales, and sounded thin and wishy-washy. None of the scenic effects worked; in exchanging the imaginative, committed staff of the Bristol Old Vic for an itinerant West End crew who'd had nothing to do with

86

putting the production together, certain unfortunate things were bound to happen. And happen they did. Within the first half-hour, a gauze had been ripped by catching it with a truck after it should have been flown out, a lighting cue had gone disastrously wrong and a large scene-shifter in braces, who became familiar as one of the leading players as the evening wore on, was discovered trundling a sofa off stage in what should have been a blackout.

I came out, I think, with an even clearer picture in my mind, by contrast, of the original. The Bristol team – and the Bristol audience – had stamped their identity on the production. Sometimes these identities are not transferable.

ELAINE WHITE

Elaine White, Christmas 1979.

I don't know who enjoyed the show more: the audience or the cast. It was John David's production of "Guys and Dolls" in the Theatre Royal, Christmas 1979. The audience watched a jolly good show, while we loved every minute on-stage and organised a round of dressing-room parties and after-show get-togethers off-stage. I was one of the Hot-Box Girls – perfect casting for the sleazy nightclub because I was always one step behind and usually looking the wrong way! But with my other wig on, I couldn't have taken my part more seriously than when I had literally to carry the flag for Sergeant Sarah Brown and her Mission Band.

Our small group of soul-savers usually entered from upstage to come into our Mission HQ through the street door. The motorised truck that carried our scenery was manoeuvred to a downstage position while we made our entrance to our signature tune of "Follow the Fold and Stray No More." There was only one time in the show when we entered instead from stage right, and during one performance this provided us with a clear view of what could have been the end of our mission.

As the mission truck trundled downstage, the scenery on it became entangled with some french flats suspended from the flies. The truck tried to keep moving, while the scenery tried to stay still. Just as the truck and the set parted company with an almighty crack, Henrietta, the DSM, made a very wise decision and brought down the iron safety curtain. What followed was a triumph of emergency planning by the production and front-of-house teams. Fred the technical stage manager surveyed the damage and said we would go up again in fifteen minutes. The actors were herded out of the way to frighten each other in the dressing-rooms with stories of what could have happened if we had been making our entrance by our usual route, i.e. exactly where two flats now lay on the floor of the stage. Meanwhile, the bar staff had been asked to stop clearing away after the interval and to start serving drinks again to the audience, who had been told that due to circumstances beyond our control there would be an extra intermission that night!

Right on time, everything was ready for us to proceed. Our prayers had been answered and we had our Mission room back again, albeit with an enormous wooden strut fixed with six-inch nails. However, knowing that we still had several entrances to make from upstage, I for one, was comforted by this addition. As usual, the audience loved the show that night, but the production and stage management team deserved a curtain call all of their own.

DAVID WOOD

The Bristol Old Vic cannot close. For all the reasons we read about. But for another reason too. Because I haven't played there yet. Twenty five years I've wanted to. Waited for the call. And I'm still waiting. I've always loved the auditorium, the atmosphere and the history, but no director has seen fit to let met tread its boards. My wife has. Jacqueline Stanbury, student at the Bristol Old Vic School in the late sixties, gave her all in a Ben Travers farce. But not me. I've come close. Recalled twice to Val May's auditions for a musical twenty years ago. But pipped at the post. Then I've had four of my children's plays performed by the Bristol Old Vic – "The Plotters of Cabbage Patch Corner" at the Little, and "The Owl and the Pussycat Went to See" . . . "The Gingerbread Man" and "Meg and Mog Show" in the New Vic. But none has yet made the main house. In early 1991 I thought I'd cracked it. An invitation to perform my "Magic and Music Show" for Easter week! Certainly! Delighted! Then the realisation that this too was for the New Vic – a smashing space to play, but not quite the real thing. So, please, please, powers that be, give me a glimmer of hope that one day I will play this historic playhouse. Keep it open!

I never think of Bristol without remembering David Horlock, who directed here in the seventies, and who introduced my writing to Bristol audiences by believing in "Plotters" and "Owl". We had been at school together in Chichester. In fact in one school play, "The Three Musketeers", David played Porthos and I played his servant, Planchet; as if that wasn't enough, future playwright Howard Brenton gave his D'Artagnan! David and I overlapped at Oxford, but only resumed our friendship here in Bristol, mainly in Renato's. David's tragic death in Salisbury last year has robbed the theatre of one of its warmest and most talented practitioners.

PEGGY ANN WOOD

My memories of the Bristol Old Vic are a kind of kaleidoscope – from their first production, "The Beaux' Stratagem".

After years of wartime, one was dazzled and delighted by the beautiful Theatre Royal, refurbished and regilded in all its glory. After one's original memories of it as "The Old Gaff" as Bristolians called it – such a down-at-heel shabby auditorium – like a beautiful woman grown old and neglected and poverty-stricken – but still beautiful.

My first appearance, in 1964, was in a riotous Denis Carey production of "Charley's Aunt" with Russell Hunter as the Aunt.

Backstage, the dressing rooms before they were rebuilt were very shabby with no running water, but cosy and full of atmosphere. I always felt I might find a stick of Mrs. Siddons' make-up as I crossed under the stage to get to the OP side.

The long tunnel entrance from King Street to the box office, was, I believe, as insignificant as possible, so that 18th-century Bristolians shouldn't be seen doing anything so wicked as going to a theatre! Now, of course, the beautiful new foyer and front of house incorporates the Coopers' Hall.

Many productions – three Hamlets, Peter O'Toole, Richard Pasco and Iain Glenn. Enchanting Christmas entertainments – the early Clinton Baddeley pantos, and Dorothy Reynolds' and Julian Slade's

90

"Christmas in King Street". The first performance in this country of Arthur Miller's "The Crucible", Timothy West in "Uncle Vanya" and, with Prunella Scales, in "A Long Day's Journey Into Night" and so many more. And, of course, the New Vic with its exciting new programme of unusual plays – of which I particularly remember the season of Irish plays.

GARY YERSHON

The theatre can be quite a dangerous place. The risks are usually artistic ones, but sometimes, cast and crew are called on to submit themselves to the mercies of the company insurance policy.

One person on a show who might be thought at little risk is the musical director. Not so. We also are in jeopardy every now and then. During a dress rehearsal of "The Three Musketeers", I was literally stunned while accompanying one of Malcolm Ransom's brilliant fights – a sword had flown out of an actor's hand, hurtled towards the pit, and hit me just above the right eye!

However, the most celebrated example of bravery on the front line concerns my distinguished colleague Neil Rhoden, musical director at the BOV for many years. Neil was at the piano, leading the band in the Act 1 finale of "Cinderella", for which I had written the score. It was an enchanting production by Chris Denys. The audience had just witnessed Fairy Godmother Pip Hinton magic up a breathtaking transformation scene. There in front of our eyes was a real white horse to pull the carriage which would take Cinders to the ball. The curtain was due to descend as the horse began its journey. But on this occasion the horse had already moved too far down the raked stage; it was tottering off balance, and listing ominously over the edge of the stage above the musicians. Neil responded superbly; he continued playing the majestic finale music with one hand, while valiantly and successfully staving off the imminent horse with the other. The audience loved it!

THE GHOST OF SARAH WHO?

There are legendary stories about ghosts at the Theatre Royal. The strongest tradition is that the ghost of the 18th-century actress Sarah Siddons walks the theatre.

Guides taking parties round can sometimes be heard to say ". . . And if you're very lucky, you may catch a glimpse of our resident theatre ghost – Sarah Siddons." But will you though? Why Sarah S?

Rifling through the history of the Theatre Royal, there is nothing to suggest she has any claim to phantasmogorical fame. The first time she worked in King Street, in March of 1779, the Bath Theatre Company had seized the opportunity of the Bristol season being finished to play a brief, unscheduled season in King Street.

Smarting from her humiliating reviews as Portia, which she had played to the daunting experience of Garrick's Shylock, she had come to Bath to learn her craft more thoroughly before chancing her reputation further on the London stage. The Bristol experiment proved a success (in spite of contravening the terms of Bristol's lease) and for the next three years she commuted from Bath to Bristol, playing up to 30 roles in a season. It must have been a punishing schedule, leaving Bristol by coach after midnight, particularly after the birth of her third child in 1779.

Exhausting though her time here must have been, it hardly forms the basis for the ghost traditions. When she left Bristol in June 1782 (after raising £106. 15s on her benefit) her loyalty to the King Street company must be in some doubt as, using her three children as her excuse to leave, she declined to appear at the subsequent benefits, at which, by that time, she would have undoubtedly proved a major box-office draw.

So where did the Sarah myth come from? Another Sarah with a far less glittering career may well hold the answer. When W. M'Cready (father of the actor W. C. Macready) took over the management of the theatre in March 1819, he brought with him from Newcastle his mistress, Sarah Desmond. They had been lovers for many years, their son, George, who was born in 1814, being passed off for some time as M'Cready's nephew. Sarah was 35 years younger than her lover and had established herself on the northern circuits as an actress of some repute. She became his leading lady in Bristol and finally, in 1821, they married.

W. C. Macready, child of William's first marriage, was only three years younger than his stepmother but it appears to have been a harmonious family, with W. C. Macready appearing many times in

Has she seen a ghost herself? Sarah Siddons strikes a dramatic pose.

Bristol. The theatre flourished under M'Cready, gas lighting was installed and the building was painted and refurbished.

In 1829 W. M'Cready died and for three years Mr. Brunton managed the theatre, Sarah continuing as leading lady. It finally went broke, and after much persuasion, "Mrs. Mac" was prevailed upon to take on the burden of the, by now, decaying building, early in 1834. With limited funds, she cleaned the theatre as best as she could, and had a new act drop and green curtain installed. Her years as manager are punctuated with respectful letters to the proprietors, asking for minimal improvements – repairs to the paintshop (then over the pit) which threatened to collapse into the auditorium under the weight of scenery, and provision for a fire in her room in the winter.

At the end of one season she made a proud curtain speech, thanking the audience for their support at a time when several regional theatres had had to close before the end of their seasons from lack of funds. In 1844 Mrs. Mac's daughter, Mazzerina (she must have got the name from a play) married James Henry Chute, who was then stage manager, thus founding a theatrical dynasty which continued in Bristol until the 1930s.

In 1843 Mrs. Mac took over the management of Bath, re-establishing an old tradition and, with the aid of her son-in-law, administered both theatres. In October of the following year, news of the death of her son, George, who had been a ship's surgeon, reached her from India. The "Very Eccentric and Sibylline Old Lady" carried on running both theatres, until her death at the age of 63 on March 8, 1852, when she was buried beside William in Bristol Cathedral.

In all 20 years of her management, she never defaulted on the rent (a rare record in those days) or failed to pay her actors on time, even if it meant paying them out of her own pocket. Surely, someone who in over 30 years, had known such joys and sorrows in the old theatre, must have some claim on its history.

Jane Cooke, head scenic artist at the Theatre Royal, who has done a considerable amount of research into Sarah M'Cready, says "Perhaps at some point the story of the two Sarahs became entangled and the more famous one emerged to fill the obligatory role of Theatre Ghost."

She adds, "For those of you who remain sceptical on the subject, there are a number of reports of a woman in black (Sarah M'Cready was a widow for 20 years) walking across the P/S fly floor towards the old offices above the auditorium and recently two flymen have heard a strange woman whispering in their ears during a show.

"Of all the nights I have worked alone in the building, one in particular stands out. I was working alone on the stage when all the lights on the P/S fly floor suddenly started swinging wildly, as if hit by an unseen hand, and continued to do so for an hour without slowing down. Not the first time this has happened. What set me thinking was – I was working in the early hours of the morning of March 8, the day "Mrs. Mac" died."

The actress June Barrie recalls being alone in the building resting after a matinée performance when she heard a woman's voice calling. She thought someone had been accidentally shut in, so she went round opening doors. Eventually she tried a door to the auditorium. "The auditorium is always hot after a performance", she says, "but when I opened the door on this occasion I was struck by a blast of ice-cold air. I just turned and ran from the building leaving everything behind – even my handbag."

Peter Harris, who worked at the theatre for years as a voluntary unpaid member of the stage crew, has another ghost story to tell.

A sighting of the ghost of Mrs. Siddons occurred in 1946. The first production by the Bristol Old Vic was "The Beaux' Strategem" in which all the cast were dressed in 18th-century costumes. In the course of the middle act, Yvonne Mitchell had to make an entrance from the OP side. To do this, she had to pass under the stage and climb the rickety staircase to the entrance at the back. During one performance, as she hurried up the stairs and paused in the wings, awaiting her cue, she was conscious of another female figure wearing a similar costume to herself also standing in the wings. Thinking no more of it, she made her entrance.

However, this little event kept nagging at her memory and so she checked up to see whether any of the other women in the cast were in the wings but realised that they were all on the other side of the stage. Later, she looked carefully at the portrait of Mrs. Siddons which hung in the front office and realised that this was how the mysterious lady had appeared to her. Thereafter she was convined that she had seen the "ghost of the Theatre Royal".

~Finale~